Interactional Family Therapy:

A
Faith-based
Perspective

Introduction to theory, practice, and
a theology of counseling and therapy

DALE F. HANSEN, *PhD, DMIN ThM*
DIANA SWIHART, *PhD, DMIN, APN CS, FAAN*

DEDICATION

This work is dedicated to my family and to those friends and clients who brought the reality of life and the ministry of a lifetime to me. It is also dedicated to the professors who were aware of the personalities of those they taught and were not afraid to teach the truth rather than being caught up in the traditional and educational cartels of this world. The many colleagues who were loyal and cared about the students they spent time teaching was reflective of their own character. Then, those I served with in the military and the many people working in that capacity to protect the freedom and wellbeing of our great country. Finally, the Practitioners who looked behind all the possibilities that cause change in people's lives in the oft times unforgiving world we live in today. -*Dale F. Hansen*

Every work, regardless of scope and size, is completed only with the help and inspiration of others. They are many and add context, depth, and relevance to the importance and continued need for exploring, supporting, and advancing the healing and strengthening of families for people of faith. This work is dedicated to my own family of faith, to my beloved husband, Stan, and my dear son and daughter-in-law, Matthew and Gianna, people of incredible faith, for their support and encouragement, and their unwavering trust in God and in me. -*Diana Swihart*

ACKNOWLEDGMENTS

I would like to acknowledge the voice of reason in my life: my wife and partner, Frankielou. -*Dale F. Hansen*

A heartfelt thanks goes to the focus groups and colleagues who volunteered their time and expertise in researching and creating this book, without whom this book would not be possible. The authors would also like to acknowledge those many others--practitioners, patients and families, speakers and teachers, and colleagues and friends who have contributed their ideas and thoughts through countless classes, seminars, lectures, and discussions we have experienced over the years. Though their names are too numerous to list, we write from their influence and want to recognize their contributions as well. To each and every one of you, thank you.

Interactive faith-based family counseling and therapy is a specialty practice by committed and compassionate practitioners. It is an honor and a privilege to serve them and to recognize their often unobserved yet significant contributions to the development and implementation of faith and spiritual care when working with individuals and families of faith. This book has emerged as our work in counseling and therapy from a faith-based perspective continues to grow, building on the experiences and insights of those at the front lines of service and practice. They are the ones who build on the past and invest themselves in the present and future of others, those who choose to serve anywhere their unique knowledge, skills, and lived experiences are needed.

A special "thank you" to Matthew Swihart who lent his own writing skills and gifts to the earlier reading and critiquing of the manuscript.

Dale F. Hansen and Diana Swihart
2020

ABOUT THE AUTHORS

Dale F. Hansen, PhD, DMin, ThM

Dale F. Hansen, PhD, DMin, ThM, is an educator, author, and consultant. He remains in private practice as a Licensed Marriage and Family Therapist and has served as a Clinical Member of the American Association of Marriage and Family Therapy (AAMFT) and the Arizona Association of Marriage and Family Therapy (AzAMFT). He is a retired Colonel in the US Army and has served as a chaplain for several law enforcement agencies. He retired after 24 years with the Federal Bureau of Investigation (FBI) in the Phoenix Division and spent his summers as a chaplain at Quantico. Dr. Hansen attended California Lutheran University with post graduate work at Arizona State University. He holds a Doctorate in Family Counseling and a Doctorate of Ministry and a Masters in Theology from Dallas Theological Seminary. He completed graduate studies at the American Institute of Family Relations and Trinity Theological Seminary. Dr. Hansen currently teaches graduate courses in Family Systems and Counseling Theory at Ottawa University in Arizona.

Diana Swihart, PhD, DMin, MSN, APN CS, NPD-BC, FAAN

Diana Swihart, PhD, DMin, MSN, APN CS, NPD-BC, FAAN, the CEO & Managing Partner for the American Academy for Preceptor Advancement, enjoys many roles in her professional career, practicing in widely diverse clinical and nonclinical settings. She currently works as a Patient Safety Nurse Consultant with the VHA National Center for Patient Safety. An author, speaker, researcher, educator, mentor, and consultant, she holds graduate degrees in nursing and leadership and doctorates in theology and ministry. She is a member of Sigma Theta Tau International (STTI), the Nurses Organization of Veterans Affairs (NOVA), the Veterans Educators Integrated Network (VEIN), a consulting partner for the Forum for Shared Governance, and several professional advisory boards. She has published and spoken on a number of topics related to nursing, shared governance, competency assessment, continuing nursing education, servant leadership, new employee orientation, professional development, building effective preceptorships and professional portfolios, business communication, and evidence-based practice in clinical settings locally, nationally, and internationally.

ORGANIZATION

Part I of this book is designed to introduce some of the ideas, concepts, and techniques underlying faith-based family therapy.

In Chapter 1, *we move beyond counseling and therapy*, looking at behavior, change agents and strategies, relationships, and how interactional faith-based therapy is defined.

Chapter 2 explores some *theories, perspectives and concepts* important for faith-based counseling and therapy practitioners to consider, such as the role of medication in therapy, the differences in apostleship and discipleship, length of treatment, history theory, and psychometric testing. Reframing and interpretation are concepts that can help the practitioner and participant change presenting problems and identify strategies for problem-solving activities. It provides a review of ahistorical, historical, and experiential approaches to counseling and therapy.

Chapter 3 then considers *therapists and theories*, briefly looking at the roles, skills, and pitfalls encountered by faith-based practitioners, going deeper into presenting problems, some perspectives of theory and technique, and the various roles of participants and practitioners in faith-based counseling and therapy.

In Chapter 4, we review the *function of interactional questions* give practitioners important tools for assessing behavior and discussing changes.

Chapter 5 discusses the *theology and ethics of therapy*, while chapter 6 reviews the treatment plans and doing therapy—therapeutic planning folded into the NEG model for interactional faith-based family therapy.

Part II provides guidelines and tools for interactional faith-based family therapy—advanced practice as we help you take the jet lag out of faith-based family therapy in chapters 7 through 9.

Chapter 7 dives into the processes of the NEG model: ***needs, expectations, and goals.*** It looks at control vs management and reviews functional and dysfunctional behaviors in family relationships and describes perception and perspective in family systems therapy.

Chapter 8 speaks to ***family relationships***, exploring individual issues and couples' issues, targeting relationships among men and women initially and then addressing issues related to children and adolescents.

Chapter 9 discusses ***faith and science***, reviewing the outcomes and recommendations from the findings of multiple focus groups looking at faith-based family therapy when implementing faith-based interactional family therapy with lessons learned and ideas for advancing concept analysis and care strategies.

Finally, in the ***epilogue***, the authors share their purpose for why a faith-based perspective and offer some final insights for effectively guiding practitioners and participants into alignment through faith-based practices in counseling and family therapy to restore healthy relationships and family systems.

What is NOT in this book?

This book will not:

- Detail the many current theories and theological battles that rage among contemporary family therapy models or argue beliefs among traditions, religions, philosophies, or world views;
- Speak to controversial or denominational issues (Swihart, 2016, xi);
- Assess the various faith-based approaches to counseling or therapy in general; or,

- Present a detailed review of literature related to research across disciplines or beliefs related to family therapies or faith-based perspectives.

Neither does this book deal with those treatments that include "buzz-words" favored in many faith-based counseling approaches and/or other forms of family therapy. While such intellectual approaches attract some teachers and practitioners, the authors are only concerned with addressing treatment effectiveness in this work. Generally, the "reality rule" of current family therapy is that the process often progresses better in books and videotapes then in reality. Do not be discouraged. Keep working and learning. You are often planting seeds that may need time and effort to germinate and produce the benefits sought through faith-based family therapy.

In conclusion, approaches and insights into family therapy are constantly developing, evolving, and maturing. This book provides a foundation for developing and advancing a faith-based perspective in interactional family therapy beyond the basic concepts and traditions. May this book provide every reader, including students and practitioners of counseling and therapy that consider themselves spiritual, find this a guide in engaging participants in the interactive processes needed to explore healing from a faith-based perspective.

TABLE OF CONTENTS

Appendices: 223

LIST OF FIGURES

PREFACE

Once we stretch our mind around a new idea, it never returns to its former shape. –OLIVER WENDELL HOLMES

When working with individuals and families of faith, the perspective of the practitioner is critical to a successful outcome. The professional techniques or personal expressions of the practitioner can either hurt or heal these vulnerable participants in the counseling or therapeutic process. This book explores an approach in initiating, facilitating, and sustaining strategic change in guiding practitioners from an interactive faith-based perspective when working with individuals and families, to applied learned professional behaviors and acquired personal wisdom as therapy in a spiritual dimension of care expressed in faith.

Integrity, trust, honesty, and faith can be reflected in changed behavior that can be observed outwardly. It is an influencing factor in how a practitioner does counseling as well as therapy when change is expected. The faith and character of the practitioner can be transparent and have a positive effect on the therapeutic process.

Therapeutic techniques, maneuvers, and interventions such as family alliances, intensifying subject matter, and emotional stability can be significant tools for a faith-based practitioner, validating the interactional process. The act of validation through faith projects belief in something that is consistent, personally relevant, and life-breathing.

Everyone believes in—has faith in—something. It could be faith in one's self, in humanity in general, or in a specific thing or person. Faith in God is the only guarantee we have found to enable us to be consistent, life-changing, and trustworthy. Conversely, having no faith leads to failed assurances with any genuine validation of consistent changed behavior if that is important to the participant client.

This manual includes some basic theory and resources for the application and improvements of therapeutic practice and approaches to engage participants in interactive faith-based processes. Though the authors are Christians, the terms operationalized in this book to describe the faith, beliefs, and practices in various traditions are intended to respect all faith traditions, not to promote any one faith tradition.

Some of the chapters contain information which—on the surface—seems redundant or repetitive. However, the unique perspectives and experiences each practitioner brings to the content provides deeper insight into what a faith-based perspective in interactional family therapy genuinely involves.

PART I.

Introduction to Interactional Family Therapy From a Faith-Based Perspective

The capacity to watch over and guard the well-being of others is an important gift, and one that is learned with great difficulty. For it is one thing to see the situation others are in, but it is quite another to care enough about them to help, and yet another to know what to do. -Judie Bopp

While *change* is traditionally the target of counseling and therapy for the client (referred to in this work as *participant*) and the counselor or therapist (referred to in this work as *practitioner*), learning a theory is often the foundation for practice in bringing about the perceived change needed in the participant through counseling/therapy sessions. However, theory is often entrenched in pedagogical reasoning, leaving the practitioner a teacher-student relationship with the participant. Is this approach to facilitating change within a therapeutic environment the best choice when providing interactional, faith-based family therapy?

When working with individuals and families in general and of faith, the perspective of the practitioner is critical to a successful outcome. The professional techniques or personal expressions of the practitioner can either hurt or heal these vulnerable participants in the counseling or therapy process. This book explores an approach to initiating, facilitating, and sustaining strategic change in guiding practitioners. Reframing the mental maps (Black & Gregersen, 2008) reflected in verbal and nonverbal communications through counseling and therapy could support the underlying change needed for developing a faith-based perspective and inform the practices frequently used as the practitioners apply learned professional behaviors and acquired personal wisdom in therapy and the spiritual dimension of care expressed in faith.

This book includes some basic theory and resources for the application and improvements of therapeutic practice and approaches to engage participants in interactive faith-based processes. For example, we will look at:

- The history and development of interactional family therapy and faith-based practices
- Basic assumptions of faith-based therapy relative to the non-pathological multiplicity of the mind and the concept of self
- Concepts of spirituality, beliefs, and faith
- Therapeutic relationships and strategic change
- Treatment options, choices, and activities
- Psychopathology and psychoeducation
- Comorbidities, complex developmental trauma, and fears
- Focus groups and workshops to guide development an analytical interpretation for the role of faith in doing therapy

What is interactional family therapy?

Understanding the composition of human beings and the language of faith are pivotal competencies for practitioners providing individual or family counseling or therapy from a faith-based perspective. *Faith* represents the beliefs and expressions of the spiritual dimension of being folded into every person, regardless of religion (belief system) or ideology. It is here the greatest change is possible. It is important that any counselor or therapist working from a faith-based perspective understands their own beliefs and spiritual needs, as well as those of their clients.

Terms such as *sin, forgiveness, redemption, reverence,* and *prayer* are often the language of faith and are expressions of the spiritual dimension. Many excellent references provide information and insight into the multitude of religious beliefs and expressions of faith experienced by others. It is not our purpose to speak to them all. In this book, the language of the spiritual dimension is expressed through faith, which becomes the objective for change by the practitioner, the human instrument of change and healing.

Iron sharpens iron, so one man sharpens another (Proverbs 27:17; NASB).

The many guiding principles of faith presented in this approach to interactional family therapy can be applied in all counseling and therapy practices with any client or client family, leading to the participants in the healing process. The scope of the faith concept in this work is specific to family therapy and builds on the care expected of all practitioners of counseling and therapy.

Resources on faith-based family therapy are virtually non-existent, especially for those professional counselors and therapists seeking to understand the faith-based perspective in therapy. This book broaches the subject of interactional faith-based family therapy and discusses its relevancy and role as well as challenges the reader with both a new perspective and the encouragement to further explore this exciting field of study.

CHAPTER 1:
Beyond Counseling and Therapy

Few are those who see with their own eyes and feel with their own hearts.
-Albert Einstein (1879-1955)

Family therapy as a practice specialty for practitioners is a recent development, having come into its own in recent years. The term *family* is not a singular unit that can be defined. It can only be operationalized to describe the interactions within a system encompassing formal consideration for homeostasis and a grounding for legal definitions by various agencies. *Family*, then, is defined legally as a group of persons who are connected by blood or by affinity or through law within two or three generations, consisting of parents and their children living together in a domestic relationship with a shared commitment to one another (USLegal).

Child behavior and most adult problems do not occur in isolation. Most child, adolescent and adult problems should be treated as family problems. The family functions as a whole and must, therefore, be viewed as a whole entity and treated for effective change to occur. *Interactional therapy* occurs when two or more individuals, such as a practitioner and a participant (individuals and/or family members), have the ability to have an effect, influence, or impact upon one another through the counseling or therapeutic process.

Interactional faith-based therapy, then, must have a reference point to give theory and techniques substance. Different faith groups offer different aspects of application, understanding, and significance to their particular faith-based theological models. The emphasis of this book is on how to remove the presenting problems that families by faith can face by altering their perspective of the problem and their patterns of interactions. The authors believe God is the Author of change, therefore, it is possible to enable families by faith to see a loving God who has accepted them totally in accordance with unfathomable grace.

Grounding faith-based interactional family therapy for practice

Basic dysfunctionality is a consequence of the essential nature of humanity and is perpetuated primarily during socialization—except in the case of neurological problems (*i.e.*, chemical and/or organic disease, congenital defects, *etc.*). An individual's aberrant behavior at any given time generally reflects the composite state of socialization within the family system, as well as the family system itself.

Frequently, person-oriented practitioners who apply individual therapy techniques to multiple family members erroneously refer to their approach as *family therapy*, which is both confusing and ineffective. To be an effective faith-based family practitioner, it is important to learn how to appropriately address the whole family as a single system for change, carefully considering the physical, psychological, and spiritual dimensions of being in how the family system functions.

How does a practitioner engage in interactional faith-based family therapy?

The theory, practice, and tools provided in this book are based on the following premises:

1. The *presenting problem* reflects the qualitative state of the immediate family system in which the identified or stated dysfunctional behavior is manifested.

2. If possible, the presenting problem must be removed to validate the process of change.

3. In all cases, the *practitioner* is responsible for facilitating the alterations of the affective behavioral and cognitive patterns of the family system to allow aberrant or dysfunctional behaviors to become unnecessary.

4. The *participant* (*i.e.*, the client family) is responsible for the positive elements of change, thereby receiving the credit for the change.

5. *God* is ultimately responsible for all lasting change (Galatians 2.20), and to Him, not the practitioner, goes the glory.

6. *Faith-based* refers to those persons, ideas, theologies, or therapeutic approaches that embrace loyalties, reverence, trust, confidence and beliefs, specifically expressed through faith and God.

7. Finally, the faith-based practitioner introduces the reality of maturity and moves the family beyond current dysfunctional behaviors to that of healthy, mature decision making. This extends to the roles of responsibility and accountability as father, mother, husband, wife, and child within the context of the family system.

What is different in interactional family therapy?

The techniques practiced today in most psychodynamic approaches tend to end family dysfunction within the uniqueness of the individual. These approaches seem to meander through sessions with no particular direction or fixed destination for the treatment, expectations, or intended outcomes. However, in Interactive Family Therapy, explicit techniques are set and measurable attempts to validate therapy with specific definable expectations for intended outcomes.

The outcomes of a theory, *per se*, are ultimately inconclusive. However, theories do generate questions to help the practitioner seek out situational and procedural information. This book builds on the following structure:

- *Therapy* identifies the needs, expectations, goals, and techniques for healing

- *Faith* expresses the perspective for the practitioner

- *Theory* (*i.e.*, the Interactional Family Therapy model) generates the questions and sets the direction and parameters of the process

- *Techniques* gather the information and address the objectives

Theories are tools for process. The interactional faith-based family therapist engenders questions specifically aimed to resolve a dysfunction within the members of a family and/or the family system.

What is the difference between counseling and therapy?

Most therapists counsel while they are doing therapy. However, not everyone who counsels is providing therapy—often they are simply giving advice or suggesting ways to improve a situation. Some of the differences between doing therapy and counseling include the following.

Counseling tends toward:

- Advice-giving

- Encouraging

- Evaluating circumstances and situations

- Exchanging information

- Suggesting/recommending alternative actions or behaviors

Therapy tends toward:

- Using creative interventions to help participants re-structure relationships

- Reframing psychological and/or spiritual problems to assist the individual or family in resolving those problems to experience healing

- Systematizing the relationships within a family objectively to allow for healing to occur epistemologically (*epistemology*, the study of the nature of knowledge, justification, and the rationality of belief and faith)

- Facilitating interactions within relationships, which is different from the more basic information gathering or advice-giving that occurs in counseling

Although in nearly all professional counseling and/or therapy sessions, social and therapeutic boundaries in counseling frequently blur or merge, the counselor or therapist defines those boundaries. In *Interactional Faith-based Family Therapy*, the therapist (practitioner) and the client's family (participants) negotiate the boundaries and define them conjointly within the context of a professional relationship and a faith perspective.

Meanwhile, the counseling community of practitioners (some in that community embracing attitudes, activities, and other practices in counseling and therapy but without a religious or spiritual basis) has struggled to comprehend the unique spiritual perspectives of its clients. Failure to recognize the differences between faith-based counseling and faith-based therapy has been both the cause and the result of ongoing conflicts among scholars and practitioners in both theology and psychology. It is in therapy that the gap closes between psychology and theology in understanding the faith-based approach. The primary problems in faith-based counseling appear to be embedded in the following limitations:

1. An inability to view counseling and therapy separately from one another and an unwillingness to collaborate;

2. An indiscriminate contempt for faith-based counseling and therapy with subsequent attempts to discredit it by many secular psychologists, therapists, and counselors;

3. A similar indiscriminate contempt for psychology with subsequent attempts to discredit it by many faith-based counseling and therapy practitioners;

4. An insistence on the integration of theology and psychology along with a failure to see that such an attempt at unification is a classic paradox when it comes to epistemology and the nature of man's beginning; and,

5. An inability to recognize safety issues and boundaries when attempting to keep a marriage solvent or a family intact.

Although advancing beyond counseling to therapy requires disentanglement from some basic counseling techniques as non-reflective, counseling remains a significant part of therapy. The dynamics of psychotherapy modeled after the historical approaches of the Austrian Sigmund Freud, a neurologist and the founder of secular psychoanalysis, have very little in common with faith-based therapy. Unfortunately, a determination to denounce all psychodynamic approaches has led many practitioners to ignore therapy and its application to people of faith. In spite of this partiality, though, some practitioners have assigned similarities to spiritual and faith-based approaches in their counseling and therapy practices. They generally define these approaches as:

- *Faith-based* approach: therapy with definite historical postulates; and,

- *Spiritual* describes therapeutic approaches to an unknown state with dynamic accountability and measurable effects or outcomes.

Correct and effective family therapy requires the practitioner to approach the family as a single yet dynamic system, recognizing how all parts of any system interact with all other parts of that system. Nothing has an isolated effect. So it is with families reflecting their levels of system health or dysfunction through learned and demonstrated behaviors of their members.

BEHAVIOR

Interactional faith-based family therapy is not a simple model of psychotherapy. Rather, it includes a fundamental paradigm shift in the study of normal and dysfunctional behaviors within families and among family members. Therefore, because behavior is contextually based, counseling and therapeutic treatments need to be contextually based, as well. Interactional faith-based family therapy recognizes how immediate environmental influences, faith, and interpersonal family relationships among family members are primary vehicles for changing behaviors relating to situations and circumstances that go beyond only counseling.

Many people come from families that adapt well to changes as they grow and learn together, facing only transitory adjustment problems. However, many problem behaviors are not pathological, disruptive, or maladjustment disorders. When they are described as such by some psychotherapists, it is often due to a difference of opinion in defining *normal* behaviors and grounded in the personal and professional beliefs of the counselor or therapist.

All behavior reflects explorations into how to be a family while meeting ethical, moral, and spiritual expectations individually and together. So often counselors and therapists are asked to fix simple problems of lived experiences related to how people within the family system communicate with one another and interact with the social environments around them, *i.e.*, school, work, church, or community services. At any given moment, the manifested behavior reveals the family system's condition in general and how well it is adapting to the pressures or forces of lived experiences encroaching upon it internally and externally.

Behavior is assumed to reflect psychosocial environmental dynamics. This implies that the environment and contextual information are altered by generic compositions coupled with current family patterns and history. Therefore, if the larger psychosocial environments are changed, in many cases, behavior will change. To the faith-based practitioner, moral values, spiritual growth and fellowship, along with personal commitment to God and others affect the individual's context. Thus, the focus moves from the individual to the individual's *context* so that at some point the individual will move philosophically from the general to the specific as they participate in interactional faith-based family therapy and going beyond "social engineering" on the part of the therapist or practitioner.

CHANGE

Change has a considerable psychological impact on the human mind. To the fearful it is threatening because it means that things may get worse. To the hopeful it is encouraging because things may get better. To the confident it is inspiring because the challenge exists to make things better.
-King Whitney, Jr.

Change in every relationship is predicated on the belief—the faith—that certain behaviors or actions will bring about a particular outcome, *e.g.*, a stronger family system with healthy members communicating and working together to meet their individual and combined needs. Each family member carries powerful *mental maps*—beliefs about cause and effect— that drive their values, expectations, plans, decisions, actions, and behaviors in response to situations and events.

Black and Gregersen (2008) describe approaches to strategic change that are relevant to interactional faith-based family counseling and therapy when family members process and act on information linked to those mental maps, building on their individual and collective lived experiences. It is critical to understand these mental maps and how they relate to individual and group thinking, acting, and driving change within familial systems for people of faith before new maps and behaviors can be considered, accepted, and adopted.

Familial relationships and individuals within those family systems are the most potent change agents in any environment or community. However, practitioners act as the primary change agents, those who promote, guide, and facilitate change among the family members and within the family system. Therapeutic techniques and tools enable practitioners to explore participants' mental maps and how they influence behaviors that are causing problems within themselves and their family systems. Change, then, must occur at the point of its greatest impact: the family. All therapeutic efforts need to be directed toward the relationships within and among families, not towards the individual alone. Successful, effective faith-based therapy and genuine changes occur first in assessing and changing mental maps and then facilitating change at multiple junctures of interaction within the family system.

Mental maps

The secret of living a life of excellence is merely a matter of thinking thoughts of excellence. Really, it's a matter of programming our minds with the kind of information that will set us free. -Charles R. Swindoll

All change—even good change—is difficult. For practitioners to facilitate change in participants and family systems, it is important to look beneath surface behaviors and discover the fundamental mental maps directing them. *Mental maps* are the maps in our heads that frame our personal views of reality and how we interact with others in our families and communities at home, school, and work. When people fail to change, they are often holding on to failed mental maps that interfere with their ability to heal and communicate accurately with others. Practitioners must capture the essence of failed change and build treatment modalities around breaking through unhealthy mental maps (sometimes called mind maps) to effect healthy changes.

Black and Gregersen (2008, p. 8) describe three questions that identify mental barriers and can help practitioners begin this process within family systems:

1. Why, when opportunities or threat stare people in the face, do people fail to see the need to change?
2. Even when people see the need, why do they often still fail to move?
3. Even when people move, why do they fail to finish—not going far or fast enough?

When practitioners and participants understand why people fail to see their need, move to address that need, and finish the work of changing from dysfunction to functional behaviors, families can break through these barriers and facilitate strategic change needed to redraw their mental maps and engage in healthy relationships.

All change begins with a history of "doing the right thing and doing it very well, but then something happens: The environment shifts and the right thing becomes the wrong thing" (Black & Gregersen, 2008, p.11). What was once the right thing or decision is now wrong, though the person still does the now wrong thing well. Practitioners see this in participants' insistence on following the old, familiar—and previously successful—mental maps resulting in an inability to change.

The practitioner introduces therapeutic techniques to guide strategic changes by helping participants see that the old right thing is now the wrong thing—the old right decisions are actually hurtful—so that they begin to see the new right thing more clearly even though they are not yet comfortable with the new way of thinking or decision-making. Over time and with patience, they become good at the new right thing. Once they master the new right thing, redrawing their mental maps to include the new right thing, the new way of thinking and behaving, they will become more comfortable in doing the new right thing well. Black and Gregersen (2008, p. 13) describe the fundamental process or cycle of strategic change in four stages:

Stage 1. Do the right thing and do it well

Stage 2. Discover that the right thing is now the wrong thing

Stage 3. Do the new right thing, but do it poorly at first

Stage 4. Eventually do the new right thing well

Once the practitioner helps the family see their need, some of the same beliefs and defense mechanisms family members may have embedded in their mental maps to protect them from anxiety or fear related to any unacceptable thoughts, feelings, beliefs, or behaviors may psychologically or spiritually stop them from moving forward. This *failure to move* becomes a brain barrier that keeps participants from working with the practitioner to explore unhealthy mental maps or responding to therapeutic techniques implemented to help them identify and begin doing the new right thing, even poorly at first. Some of the same defense mechanisms and broken mental maps that can stop participants from seeing their need can also influence their inability to move.

Finally, once familial participants see their need and begin to move forward in their therapy to develop new mental maps to change dysfunctional or problematic behaviors, they still *need to finish* their work, continuing to strengthen their faith and relational skills until they are able to do the new right things (*i.e.*, engaging in healthy decision making and situationally appropriate behaviors) and doing them well. Interactional faith-based family therapy focuses on helping participants create and expand healthy mental maps and break through the brain barriers interfering with their abilities to communicate and interact with one another in mutually respectful and spiritually healing ways.

Change is constant and frequently becomes a key stressor that drives people to behave in dysfunctional ways. Often, practitioners serve as change agents to help participant families navigate change processes strategically towards anticipating and managing change rather than feeling forced to react to crises or situations perceived to be outside of their control, for example. Practitioners help remove the brain barriers and facilitate wholeness and relational health by therapeutically guiding them in reframing newer and healthier mental maps.

Change agents

Couros (2013) described five characteristics of a change agent also seen in interactional faith-based practitioners of family therapy: clear vision, patient yet persistent, asks tough questions, is knowledgeable and leads by example, and builds strong relationships on trust. What do these characteristics look like in faith-based family therapy?

Clear vision. Although there are multiple ways to do something, other approaches to change, the practitioner or participant with the clear vision of what is needed to bring about healing is usually the one who can guide the family toward a common purpose for change and relational health.

Patient yet persistent. Practitioners ensure that all forward movements are towards the agreed upon treatment outcomes, are effectively contributing to the relational health of familial participants and are actively facilitating participants' ability to draw new mental maps for improving previously dysfunctional behaviors.

Asks tough questions. Practitioners ask questions that focus therapy on the decisions and behaviors that brought the family members to seek help. They guide participants in making their own conclusions about their decisions and accepting ownership for their behaviors. Practitioners keep asking questions to help participants think, challenge their current mental maps, and explore the barriers to change that may be driving their dysfunctional behaviors. We will explore these questions later in the book when we discuss functions and interactional questions as tools for assessing behavior and discussing changes.

Knowledgeable and leads by example. Practitioners seeking to facilitate change in faith-based families must know and understand their own faith and practice the behaviors they are teaching their participants. For example, if practitioners complain about their own relationships with their families, distrust or deny God, or place their faith only in themselves, participants may question their ability to help them through their relational problems, to address their dysfunctional behaviors, or to remove the barriers needed to change unhealthy mental maps and improve their family systems.

Strong relationships built on trust. So often family members have difficulty trusting one another—or anyone who might be trying to help them. Practitioners begin by establishing a relationship built on trust and mutual respect. Frequently the practitioner will share the same or a similar faith as the participants. Shared beliefs can strengthen the practitioner's ability to connect with participants in interactional faith-based family therapy. It must be stated at the beginning when practitioners do not share the faith or beliefs of the participants and give them an opportunity to remain in therapy with them or to choose another practitioner who can provide faith-based family therapy grounded in the shared beliefs that influence their ethical, moral, and spiritual mental maps to drive healthy behavioral changes.

Agents of change (or *change agents*) are those individuals who demonstrate these characteristics to engage in a therapeutic partnership with one another to facilitate building mental maps directing healthy behaviors to be experienced in relational interactions. The key concepts are faith-based and focus on accurate communication and respectful relationships to overcome resistance to change. Black and Gregersen (2008) recognized how people are wired to resist random changes, to survive, and so to hold on to whatever perceived stability or sameness has worked for them previously.

This can be seen in how individuals making poor relationship decisions often return again and again to the behaviors that supported those decisions. If there is no change in the mental maps, there will be few if any real or lasting change in behaviors.

Practitioners seek to help the participants in family systems to redraw their mental maps and build new relationships by changing dysfunctional or problematic behaviors and improving how they interact with their family members and others. Unless practitioners can move the family from an unhealthy relational model, they are essentially doing individual counseling and therapy with multiple people present using approaches that often reject or fail to consider the established spiritual and emotional mental maps of faith.

RELATIONSHIPS

Therapy in interactional faith-based family therapy focuses on relieving emotional and spiritual pain by addressing psychosocial problems within the family systems and relationships of people using faith as a catalyst. It involves at least two fundamental elements: a therapist (or *practitioner*) and a therapeutic relationship. The family practitioner does not require the entire family to be present during therapy sessions. Only those family members necessary to alter or change the processes influencing the presenting problem identified at the beginning of the therapeutic relationship are needed. The perspectives of key family members are usually more important than the quantity or number of family members attending a session.

Whenever possible, though, having multiple family members present initially allows the practitioner greater opportunity to observe relevant and non-relevant patterns of behavior within the family system. The practitioner looks for interactional patterns that permit the greatest leverage within the relationships which can be used therapeutically to facilitate healing.

However, an individual does not necessarily need another person to form a relationship resulting in dysfunctional or problematic behavior. An individual could be reacting to a *myth* (a belief which cannot be supported by fact, *e.g.*, a legend, fiction, tradition, epic, or fable) folded into a faulty mental map. For example, a family member may displace or project the attributes of an earthly parent or spouse onto their image of a heavenly Father, or conversely, those of a heavenly Father onto an earthly parent or spouse. Therapy is guided towards altering the relationship between the individual and the myth, in many cases allowing the dysfunctional behavior to become unnecessary and redrawing the mental map. Sometimes, though, people prefer to hold onto their myths, so they can excuse their behaviors or failures to move by declaring, "*I cannot do that because...*"

Behavior that constitutes the *presenting problem*, the concern or dysfunction which brings the person or family into therapy, with the *Identified Person* (the one believed to be exhibiting or causing the problematic or dysfunctional behaviors; sometimes referred to as the *Identified Patient* in psychodynamic therapies using a medical model) are both general and non-relevant. The Identified Person is the person established by the family as the source of the problems—the "dysfunctional" one in the family. However, it is function rather than the specific behavior that draws the attention of the family practitioner. What works or does not work for most participants depends on what gets noticed. Therefore, it is important for the practitioner to see most *behavior* as necessary and generally normal, even when problematic, rather than as abnormal.

Problematic behaviors occurring after previously unsuccessful counseling or therapy and prior to the time of referral or initiation of therapy are of interest in that they, too, may influence the participants' functioning, readiness to change, and ability to form a therapeutic relationship with a new practitioner. Facilitating successful changes in dysfunctional or problematic behaviors and remapping those changes to new and healthier mental maps within the context of faith and healed familial relationships encompass the objective and expected outcomes of faith-based family therapy.

IN CONCLUSION

Interactional faith-based family therapy involves any attempt to modify salient environmental features, most importantly, interpersonal contracts or beliefs about those contracts that alter interactional behavior patterns and shift disruptive mental maps. This process allows the presenting problem to become unacceptable to the client family members, thereby internalizing the willingness for them to be spiritually, emotionally, and behaviorally healthy.

This approach to family therapy, then, implements social, emotional, spiritual, and behavioral negotiation to achieve expected outcomes. It involves: (a) assessing what the family members need to normalize their family system; (b) exploring how the family members express behavioral expectations; and, (c) determining the direction in which to alter behaviors and mental maps to meet those needs and expectations.

Once clarity and agreement have been reached, the practitioner helps modify the family system or structure and encourages the presenting problem to become unacceptable to the family members. This simultaneously alters interactional participant patterns, relationships and beliefs about the family system. Simply stated, the practitioner engages the family at the point or level of establishing a relationship—not as a specialist working externally and from a distance—and facilitates adjustments in how the various familial relationships are enacted in a healthier manner while observing participants' relational behaviors and expressions of faith, trust, and hope.

This chapter provided a general overview of the thinking that supports interactional faith-based family therapy. Central to interactional family therapy is the relationship, not the individual being treated. *Relationships* are identified as patterns of behavior that occur between individuals or myths individuals are interacting with at any time. The most difficult part of becoming an effective interactional faith-based family practitioner is encouraging a paradigm shift from working within an individual problem and working with relationships involving unnecessary behavior between or among family members. All behavior is assumed to be within the context that determines the therapeutic approach sustained by faith and trust in the therapist. The perspective for therapy is more important than the number of people present in the family therapy session.

It must be noted here that while family therapy is not effective in altering the prognosis for biochemically-based disorders, it can support standard pharmacological treatments. Sometimes, practitioners work with physicians and participants on medications that can hasten the process of healing or create change when coupled with family therapy (see Chapter 2).

CHAPTER 2:

Theories, Perspectives and Concepts

*Once we stretch our mind around a new idea, it never returns
to its former shape.* -Oliver Wendell Holmes

THEORIES AND MODELS

A brief introduction to the development of theory and models of family
therapy provides practitioners with a necessary background for an accurate perspective of current theories and concepts of counseling and therapy. The brief snapshots of these approaches to therapy included in this
chapter also offer some context and opportunities for interactional faith-
based family therapy practitioners to engage with other professionals to
continually improve learning and services for families of faith. When faith-
based family practitioners consider how professional counseling activities
and psychotherapies have progressed over time, they can advance their
own successes through collaborative referrals when necessary, *e.g.*, when
participants in therapy also require (a) extensive individual therapy; (b)
medication or medical management of underlying diseases or disorders;
or, (c) legal counsel.

Historical, ahistorical, and experiential approaches and techniques

Family systems therapists concur that families are comprised of interlocking subunits that influence the presenting problems targeted for correction or healing, yet each unit or subunit works differently from others. Family systems therapeutic approaches can be roughly divided into three categories: (a) historical, (b) ahistorical, and (c) experiential (Levant, 1984). Let's expand these categories a bit and look at them more closely within the context of faith-based family therapy.

HISTORICAL APPROACHES

The *historical* approach to counseling or therapy is sometimes referred to as *traditional* or *past-oriented* therapy. It has several common characteristics: (a) psychoanalytic roots; (b) individual and individualization focus; (c) long-term therapy required; and, (d) passive methodology. They are evidenced in the multiple theories of psychopathology and techniques to encourage behavior change seen in many counseling and therapy practices today.

Historical models often focus more on the intrapersonal dynamics of the individual rather than interpersonal, relational interactions among family members. To date, although these historical models have consistently failed to produce empirical evidence of genuine or sustainable effectiveness, two approaches still seen in family therapy included in this chapter as examples of historical approaches are Object Relations Family Therapy and Multigenerational Family Therapy.

Object Relations family therapy

Object relations theory emphasizes the role of an object in psychological processes, *i.e.*, other people or elements of others, primarily an individual's parents or primary caregiver. Specifically, it is about "intrapsychic activity based on the internalization of functional aspects of the experience of others and how they relate to one another in an individual's mind" (Mills, 2010, Abstract). The principle of this historical psychoanalytic model used to treat families is grounded in object relations and how adults relate to others and situations based on early family interactions and experiences. The practitioner's primary goal, for example, is to have participants work through how each one projects onto the other family members' persona based on past relationships, usually during infancy and childhood. The practitioner remains neutral, allowing the participant to work through him or her to develop more mature defense mechanisms for interacting with family members. Techniques emphasize psychic development and insight and focus on early figures of attachment and dependency.

Multigenerational family therapy

Murray Bowen's *Multigenerational Family Therapy* (Friedman, 1991), though similar to object relations therapy in some respects, focuses on exploring how participants' current problems may be rooted in genera-tional patterns. The primary differences are the additional emphasis on facts related to a multigenerational transmission of pathology on an indi-vidual rather than considering the participant families' thoughts, beliefs, emotions, or relational behaviors. Bowen's approach embraced four basic constructs: (a) differentiation, (b) emotional system, (c) multigenerational transmission, and (d) emotional triangle.

Practitioners often create *familograms* or *genograms*, family maps where interpersonal and transgenerational processes are discovered and analyzed. These historical processes are then examined with families to show differentiations and patterns impacting their current behaviors. Techniques are then employed to help the family develop functional behav-iors, end emotional isolation, and manage anxiety, for example.

James Framo and others further advanced this approach as Inter-generational Family Therapy for marriage and family therapy practi-tioners. Framo believed it was as important to know what was happening with people intra-personally as it was interpersonally. He believed many problems in life can be traced to a participant's family-of-origin, *e.g.*, individuals live through and repeat with family members the conflicts that occurred in their families of origin, repeating itself from one generation to the next (Essays, 2018). Practitioners address relevant problems but also trace these intergenerational problems back to their familial roots. Techniques include creating and analyzing family maps, assessing the family history of participants, and discovering how ancestral behaviors drive current family dynamics and issues.

Theories of psychopathology and behavior change

Psychopathology (the study of mental or behavioral disorders) and behavior-change theories and techniques are quite different among the various psychotherapies. In traditional, historical models, the individual (IP) has a core intrapersonal problem residing within his or her mind and personality. This person may lack appropriate coping or adaptive skills (*behaviors*), have skewed or irrational thinking linked to faulty mental maps (*cognition*), or be developmentally limited or unable to resolve internal conflicts (*psychodynamic*) without assistance. The individual seemingly operates in a psychological contextual vacuum (*i.e.*, the "inner child" struggling mentally and emotionally because of unresolved past events or traumas).

At times, traditional models have been referred to as *medical models*, treating mental and behavioral disorders as physical diseases that may require medication and other medical procedures administered by physicians or *psychiatrists* (medical physicians specializing in the diagnosis and treatment of mental and behavioral disorders). The intangible emotional, mental, or spiritual problems within the individual are diagnosed and treated in the same manner as a tangible physical disease in the heart or spleen or any other organ of the body, *i.e.*, chemical dependency or addiction.

When presenting for interactional faith-based family therapy, regardless of underlying mental or physical diseases or disorders in the IP, the practitioner's basic premise for care is: *Behavior at any given time reflects the quality of the system in which it exists.* From a systems perspective, then, the presenting problem that influences relevant behavior can fluctuate as the system changes or moves to a different member within the family unit. Family therapy provides information about the system and the family structure and organization. For example, failure to change a presenting problem may result from resistance to change due to personal insecurities. Either the individual IP or the family members may not want patterns of behavior to change, even though the IP or family members may say otherwise. Sometimes, family members become more comfortable with the dysfunction than in trying to adapt to change, even healthy change.

Intrapersonal and interpersonal models

Interactional faith-based family practitioners do not ignore the *intrapersonal* struggles that take place within the person or the impact of learned behaviors from previous generations. Rather, they move beyond the intrapersonal to work conjointly with *interpersonal* changes that occur between and among individuals within the family system or unit in the present. Interpersonal models focus on patterns of behavior, not specifically on the past events or on any intrapersonal deficits. The focus of therapy is specifically on the participant determined by the family to be the Identified Person (IP) causing the dysfunction within the family unit. This is often the person family members seek counseling or family therapy to 'fix'.

Interactional faith-based family therapy is an interpersonal model using the family systems theory and focusing on treating the relationships (*structure*) within a family unit. Other forms of psychotherapy are generally based on intrapersonal (or *deficit*) models when they focus on individual discrepancies or dysfunctions. The individual deficit approach is the traditional psychotherapeutic treatment approach, which is often identified with Freudian psychology with Sigmund Freud being one of its strongest representatives. His theories have been among the first and easiest to modify when defining specific psychodynamic approaches to traditional *secular* (having no religious or spiritual basis) or *humanistic* (stressing the potential value and goodness of human beings with focus primarily on human responses rather than divine or supernatural matters) in counseling and therapy. The practitioner generally uses various methods to explore an individual's past to resolve human problems rationally, often dismissing spiritual concerns or resources accessed through faith as being unnecessary or even irrational.

AHISTORICAL APPROACHES

The *ahistorical,* or process, *approach* attempts to remove the presenting problem by altering family interactional patterns of behavior. The current ways of interacting with one another may or may not be related to the presenting problem but certainly causes it to continue. The ahistorical process approach has four characteristics:

1. *Present orientation*—history of the presenting problem is all that is needed

2. *Focus remains on overt behavior* with emphasis on the current belief system as a tool for leverage

3. *Alters patterns of interactions* through the recipient as well as determining the behavior of others

4. *Active and directive* in session that assumes compliance and change

Practitioners adhering to the ahistorical process select their systems approach from one or more of four models: (a) communication, (b) structural and strategic, (c) behavioral, and (d) psychoeducational. There are depths and overlaps within and among these models that go beyond the scope of this book. However, the following brief overviews can help practitioners of faith-based interactive therapy consider the best strategies for treating individuals and family systems when working with process approaches.

Communication models: MRI, Strategic, and Milan

This model is not a single therapeutic approach but does share a core of common characteristics. Systems' thinking in the communication models requires detailed analysis of presenting problems, identification of resulting behavior patterns, and alterations of relevant interactions by practitioners with their participants.

Mental Research Institute (MRI) is the most well-known organization for employing communication models. The institute was established by Don D. Jackson and colleagues for studying brief and family therapy in the fields of interactional/systemic studies, psychotherapies, and family therapy in 1959. Their communication models are represented in the works of Virginia Satir, Gregory Bateson, Jay Haley, John Weakland, and others (Fisch, Weakland, & Segal, 1982). The roles of these practitioners are based on the experience and levels of their own delivery and skills. The techniques focus on reframes to get a shift in participant perspective and compliance. Many of the techniques were derived from Milton Erickson's work in reimagining traditional theories, models, and strategies, *i.e.*, covert or conversational hypnosis.

The *Strategic Family Model*, introduced by Jay Haley (1987), refers to any therapy that is brief, problem-focused, and dependent on an active practitioner. Haley integrated the concepts of MRI and Milton Erickson to build his model of Structural Family Therapy. Practitioners use behavioral techniques to change family and dyadic interactions (*e.g.*, the husband-wife relationship). The presenting problem is altered to make it amenable to modification of behavioral sequences.

Techniques of reframing, using *paradoxes* (self-contradictory state-ments, propositions, or seemingly illogical ideas that eventually prove to be appropriate or true), and getting participants to pretend to change initially characterize the strategic model. The paradox usually requires the practi-tioner to exaggerate the problem behavior so change can be restrained. For example, a parent's adult son is an alcoholic. The practitioner insists that the parent should bail him out and provide him with care because that is his or her "Christian duty." The practitioner's intent is that the parent would become angry with the therapist and respond oppositely by allowing the son to face the consequences of his addiction and inappropriate behaviors.

The *Milan (Systematic) Model* is the truest family adaptation to the systems perspective approach of all the communication models. However, it involves too many resources to make it practical in most practice envi-ronments for counseling and family therapy. Milan family practitioners use systematic techniques to alter the dysfunctional family patterns by inducing circular questioning, positive associations, counter paradoxes, and task assignments to facilitate problem resolution and behavior change. Practitioners maintain a neutral position while asking questions to reduce or eliminate giving the family any cues against which to react (*e.g.*, "When your child behaves in an appropriate manner, does that make you want to support him?"). Such techniques for introducing information into the fam-ily system and thereby altering interactions are basic to the Milan model.

Structural Family Therapy

In *Structural Family Therapy*, practitioners seek to change family patterns through in-session manipulation of healthy and problematic family inter-actions. This approach assumes that dysfunctional behavior reflects an inadequate structure within the family system. Salvador Minuchin devel-oped this approach based on his assumptions about interactions and sys-tems (Minuchin & Fishman, 1981; Minuchin, Reiter, & Borda, 2014). This therapy is action-oriented and attempts to alter the presenting problem as the goal of therapy. Practitioners refocus attention from the Identified Person (IP) to the family as a unit, responding to family members using humor and action to determine where in the system the structure fails to carry out its functions.

Therapeutic techniques typically include making the family feel comfortable, task setting, re-enactment of the problem so the therapist can use information for change, and reframing and *joining*, an essential way of creating therapeutic alliances and healthy working relationships within the family. For example, a child is distracting the participant family's therapy session. Recognizing the presenting problem to be the child's acting-out behavior, the practitioner ignores the child and instead asks the parents, "How long do you plan to allow that [child's distracting behavior] to continue?"

Behavioral Models

The behavioral model for children assumes that behavior reflects a learned response. Although often criticized for being linear because of its emphasis on the analysis of antecedents, consequences, and contingencies of the problem behavior, it falls well within the thinking of contemporary family therapy. Practitioners function as consultants to parents and seek to design a behavioral fit that best reflects the parents' ability to implement the desired change. Techniques include timeouts, behavioral modeling, prompting, shaping, problem-solving, contracting, *etc.*, are all interactional methods for working with children.

The *Cognitive Behavioral Model* (CBT)—one of the most popular models today—tends to attract practitioners and participants with moral agendas and pre-set theories about marriages and families. CBT is marginally effective when employed as an Ahistorical or Historical approach to family or systems therapy. It is frequently seen in practice when practitioners teach skill development and is often a preferred methodology by many authors of "Self Help" books.

Psychoeducational Model

Within the last decade, clinicians have begun treating schizophrenic clients and their families using an education-based model. By teaching families about schizophrenia, stress can be reduced. The therapist has the multifaceted role of therapist, teacher, consultant and liaison to the medical field. Techniques are in basic skill building and some Structural Family Therapy approaches in sessions.

EXPERIENTIAL THERAPY MODELS

Experiential therapy is a model using expressive tools and activities to recreate, re-enact, or re-experience events from past or present relational interactions and movement rather than the more traditional historic practitioners' emphasis on talk therapy (Mahrer, 2004). Techniques include such activities as role-playing and guided imagery. Practitioners provide various props to enhance the experiences, such as music, art, and animals. When they work with families, therapy is characterized by an emphasis on the participant's individual growth, self-development within the family unit, and engagement in the lived experiences of the therapeutic process. During the sessions, each participant is taught healthy expressions of emotion, spontaneity, appropriate response, and how to be responsible for self through their experiences and interactions with one another.

Although the Gestalt approach developed by Fritz Perls in 1912 claims to be family therapy, it is essentially individual oriented therapy that tries to explain perceptions as an organized whole rather than as the sum of their parts. Family units are comprised of multiple members who are more than or different from one another individually and in combination within the family system. Gestalt psychotherapy is a participant-centered approach that focuses the participant on the present, seeking to understand what is occurring now to gain insight into his or her behaviors and relationships, and to accept personal responsibility for his or her decisions and behaviors (Mann, 2010).

Carl Whitaker, a traditionally trained psychiatrist, was a pioneer in experimental psychotherapy. Cag and Acar (2015) examined his basic concepts and principles of symbolic-experiential family therapy as expressed in the movie *Ya Sonra*. Their study describes an excellent example of family therapy from an experiential approach: "Emotional deadness, pathology as a symptom of development, the focus person of the problem in the family, marriage greater than its parts, blind marriage, flexibility of roles, the role of therapist, seeing family and client, the objectives of therapy, and the techniques used in therapy are among the theoretical concepts of symbolic-experiential family therapy" (Abstract, p.575).

Eventually, Virginia Satir became more experiential in her later years, although more visual and less symbolic in her techniques than Whitaker (Satir, Banmen, Gerber, & Gomori, 1991). Practitioners model the skills advocated, such as sharing feelings, exploring fantasies, confronting behaviors and faulty mental maps, and demonstrating caring. Techniques involve everything from drama activities to use of ropes and blindfolds for building trust, for example. Many practitioners with high profile personalities have increased the popularity of experiential models are and expanded this approach in doing individual and family therapy.

HOW DOES INTERACTIVE FAITH-BASED FAMILY THERAPY DIFFER?

Practitioners who insist on calling up the past usually do so because of clinical training and learned psychodynamic theories such as those seen in these brief examples. These approaches usually focus on personality and see human behavior as reflections of conscious and unconscious forces in one form or another. This seems to work for them because the questions they ask participants are subjectively interpreted to confirm the hypotheses they formed initially to generate the questions explored during therapy.

In this way, they validate whichever theory they choose to use in practice through *circular reasoning*, a logical fallacy that assumes what the therapist is attempting to explain or prove.

Interactive faith-based family practitioners use a similar approach to therapy seen in historical and experiential methods as a *process of elimination*, logical methods for considering and rejecting possible choices or decisions through questioning, usually until only one probability, option, or decision remains. Their approach is *ahistorical*, not relying on responses to past behaviors but redirecting interactive processes toward the present and future through reframing and interpretation to align mental maps with functional and healthy behaviors individually and within the family unit.

Unlike the approaches seen in psychodynamic theories, the *family systems therapy approach* helps participants resolve their issues or problems within the context of individual and group dynamics within the family unit. This approach as used by interactive faith-based family practitioners often asserts that the technique of recalling past events has limited value for changing current problematic behavior or faulty mental maps.

There are no enduring regrets or specific needs to re-invent or rationalize past behavior to change present and future behavior unless poor behavior is first differentiated and linked to troublesome mental maps needing to be amended. Thus, there are generally no "why" questions in therapy because, in a sense, asking them seems to justify those previous behaviors. For example, *forgiveness* is a present action for a past event that cannot be accessed or reclaimed as an excuse for indulging in unhealthy behavior.

In most historical models wherein personal deficits are emphasized, practitioners believe delving into the past to find the beginnings and development of a deficit or dysfunction somehow helps them restore or repair that dysfunction by identifying or acknowledging it as a starting point for therapy. In faith-based therapy, practitioners and participants recognize there will always be consequences of decisions and actions in life regardless of when they began.

Traumatic events and their consequences, in time, can paralyze people, leading them to create distortions in their thinking and ways of behaving to protect themselves. People naturally build *defense mechanisms* (mental tactics intended to reduce or avoid anxiety or emotional conflicts arising from unacceptable feelings or thoughts; *e.g.*, projection, denial, rationalization, humor, repression, regression, displacement, acting out, or intellectualization) to help them temporarily ease the stress or pain of an event or to adapt to an anxiety-provoking situation.

For example, appropriate *humor* can help relieve a stressful moment or help one look at a situation from another perspective. People refusing to acknowledge a problem or situation may be in *denial*. Some people cope with their problems by *acting out* rather than reflecting on their feelings or decisions leading to their current difficulties. Occasionally people will go back to previous ways of responding to stress or anxiety, *regressing* to an earlier, more successful way of dealing with their problems. Although defense mechanisms can be a form of self-deception or a way of hiding from reality, they can also be temporary adaptive techniques for time needed for managing difficult situations or crises.

Faith-based practitioners help participants see how the healing energy to face those events and consequences come from the faith to confront and let go of what cannot be changed and to let a resolute faith in God—in something bigger than the visible—help them make lasting changes that heal and strengthen them individually and as family units.

PERSPECTIVES AND CONCEPTS

Before a practitioner can effectively and practically disentangle the numerous theories and strategies for successful faith-based counseling and therapy it is important to differentiate some of the multiple and diverse concepts and perspectives related to faith within psychological or psychosocial approaches. The history of therapy and philosophical beliefs of practitioners and participants are folded into past and current theories of practice.

As we move further into interactive faith-based family therapy, professional counseling will be defined and integrated into therapeutic principles and treatment activities, whether it is repeatedly stated or not. The focus of the remainder of this work, then, will be on clarifying counseling and therapeutic perspectives, concepts, perceptions of faith and belief, individual and family strategies and activities, and targeted outcomes. Let's begin by looking briefly at a few traditional approaches of psychotherapy and faith-based family therapy.

The dynamics in *psychotherapy* for treating behavioral and mental disorders through psychological means rather than medically were modeled after the historical approaches of Sigmund Freud, Alfred Adler, and Carl Jung and have little in common with faith-based perspectives in counseling or therapy. The primary relationship is between the practitioner and an individual participant in a psychoanalytic relationship. Treatment revolves around explorations of the mental maps hidden in the unconscious mind that are influencing or directing participants' current behaviors and decisions.

The British Psychoanalytic Council (Milton, 2014) published an excellent booklet on *Making Sense of Psychotherapy and Psychoanalysis* that briefly explains the main approaches and differences in various types of psychotherapy. Milton describes psychotherapy as "conversations with a listener who is trained to help you make sense of, and try to change, things that are troubling you. It is something you take an active working part in, rather than something you are just prescribed or given, such as medication" (p.3).

Over time, the many different approaches to psychotherapy generally grounded in individual practitioner's philosophies, perspectives, and faith (or declared lack of or rejection of faith) espoused by practitioners have evolved into a few basic types: (a) behavioral and cognitive therapies; (b) person-centered and other humanistic therapies; (c) psychoanalytic and systems therapy; and, (d) integrated or combined therapies. Participants are treated individually, in couples, or in groups. Families often fall into the category for 'group' therapy unless the practitioner specifically works with families.

Therapy often begins by selecting and examining an Identified Person (*i.e.*, the one with a presenting problem, or one who has been demonstrating aberrant or dysfunctional behaviors). Practitioners assess what individuals or family members (participants) believe conceptually, how their behaviors impact themselves and others relationally, and how they might change those behaviors, *e.g.*, through cognitive behavioral therapy (CBT) or psychoanalysis. CBT uses structured dialog and journaling to help participants increase personal and situational awareness, focusing on challenging and redrawing distorted mental maps, increasing emotional stability, and building coping strategies targeting real or perceived problems for resolution.

Though frequently differing in underlying beliefs and practices of psychotherapy, the general effectiveness of faith-based counseling and therapy has been demonstrated in practice regardless of which psychotherapeutic theory or counseling approach is followed. The pervasive impact of faith as a catalyst to actively redraw mental maps, to change dysfunctional and aberrant behaviors, and to bring healing often confuses those therapists or practitioners who have historically labeled faith as an unknown or unknowable phenomenon in effecting an initial or sustainable life change in participants. It is important, then, to explore some perspectives and concepts important for interactive therapies for all practitioners engaged in treating people of faith struggling with mental maps twisted by real or imagined fears, depression, anxiety and stress, and disruptive behaviors interfering in their relationships with their God, their families, and others regardless of their own underlying philosophies or perspectives.

Philosophy, the study of the fundamental nature of knowledge, reality, existence, religion, and experience, often informs the inherent beliefs and expressions of faith of many practitioners and participants. Philosophies are embedded in how people build the mental maps that guide their thinking, reasoning, judgment, and behavior. People are often more comfortable talking about their philosophies rather than discussing the deeper truths of their faith perspectives or relationships with—or without—God.

Perspectives expressed in this book refer to the faith-based attitudes, viewpoints, positions, approaches, and interpretations of behaviors and how God helps practitioners and participants correct and strengthen their mental maps therapeutically. A *perspective*, then, is an attitude or way of respecting the beliefs of participants and folding faith into therapy.

Interactive faith-based family therapy requires three basic perspectives when helping participants achieve emotional stability and mental and spiritual balance within the deeper contexts of faith and relationship: (a) clarity of personal issues; (b) recognition of personal needs; and, (c) the ability to collaborate expectations and goals.

Clarification of personal issues begins and proceeds on the foundation of conceptual reality, recognizing human beings exist for the distinct purpose of *relationship*, which is described in faith-based therapy as the way in which two or more individuals are connected and interact with one another. The most fundamental relationship is between an individual and God. Even if one chooses to reject God, he or she acknowledges a dysfunctional relationship with God or with the idea of God based on how his or her faith is expressed in belief or unbelief. Family relationships function within a basic unit of male and female which may expand to include children, parents, and others. Through multiple and diverse interactions and within the context of relationship, participants learn to recognize and negotiate their personal needs and collaborate expectations and goals for themselves and their families.

Participants develop a therapeutic relationship with their practitioner within which they can reflect on dysfunctional or hurtful behaviors, personal and family relationships, and engage in strategies to help them gain insight and healing for themselves and their families. *Clarity (i.e.,* the quality of being logical and understandable, certain or definite, and transparent) of personal issues first requires a mutual acknowledgement of the continuum of human behaviors, beliefs, and concepts of faith, morality, personal responsibility, and healthy relationships by practitioners and participants in therapy. A participant in faith-based family therapy accepts a consistent framework and perspective that follow these counseling and therapeutic approaches to emotional stability and mental and spiritual balance grounded in functional and healthy relationships.

Sheppard defines *professional counseling* as "the skilled and principled use of relationship to facilitate self-knowledge, emotional acceptance and growth and the optimal development of personal resources… to provide an opportunity to work towards living more satisfyingly and resourcefully. Counselling relationships will vary according to need but may be concerned with developmental issues, addressing and resolving specific problems, making decisions, coping with crisis, developing personal insights and knowledge, working through feelings of inner conflict or improving relationships with others. The counsellor's role is to facilitate the [participant's] work in ways that respect the [participant's] values, personal resources and capacity for self-determination" (Gladding, 2004, p.6).

In this context, the concept of professional counseling used in family therapy is the process of using skills to instigate a changed life by demonstrating truth and clarity to a person with an identified problem without knowing or being sure of their true needs in life. It usually assumes a psychological and/or medical framework that may incorporate some faith-based principles and activities. Interestingly, behavioral therapy does not deny the validity of various aspects of psychotherapy or of medical approaches to counseling in mental health care when using approaches consistent with expressions of faith at the same time.

Faith-based family practitioners combine the application of professional counseling skills with the therapeutic tools and activities necessary for helping family members reframe their problems, redraw dysfunctional or problematic mental maps, and modify troublesome behaviors. Change emerges in a safe environment that facilitates emotional and spiritual healing within relationships and in accordance with a shared worldview unlimited by *collaborative engagement*, a modality used among people with shared expectations and goals. This intentional restorative approach to interactive faith-based family therapy allows practitioners and participants with different ideas, beliefs, or opinions to engage in seeking resolutions emotionally, spiritually, and behaviorally.

Treatment approaches and techniques for people of faith work toward establishing expectations and helping participants embrace faith-based goals. Practitioners actively seek to move participants toward realistic, supported, and achievable changes in their mental maps and behaviors, preferably without medication. The emphasis is on reframing and strengthening participants' relationships with amended mental maps, altered behaviors, and revised familial structures to improve personal well-being and behavioral interactions among family members. The ultimate goal lies in enhancing personal, spousal, and familial relationships through faith-based interactions and responses to problems and change without compromising their values, beliefs, or personal or professional boundaries.

MEDICATION

Shelly, John, and others (1983) note that dysfunctional responses can result from the effects of sin, the belief that a person of faith has somehow missed the mark of what is spiritually and socially acceptable behavior (*i.e.*, an immoral act that transgresses divine law or rebels against God's directives; as noted in 1 John 3.4, Deuteronomy 9.7, and Joshua 1.18, for example). Such a response in people of faith can manifest itself in many forms of suffering, including anxiety, anger, fear, despair, alienation, spiritual distress, behavioral changes, overwhelming feelings of guilt, and even in suicidal thinking.

People of faith generally believe that God's grace is needed to overcome the effects of sin. His grace is appropriated through faith, or faithfulness. As such, faith is more than an inner conviction or belief in some vague idea of God or reliance on unclear spiritual principles. Faith that is drawn upon in interactive faith-based family therapy is a steadfast reliability and trust in God, a foundation for what is hoped for within the context of proving or testing invisible realities. Though they often do so imperfectly, people of faith live in steadfast reliability on God, bearing witness to scriptural Truth that frames their mental maps, informs their decisions, and guides their behaviors.

Faith is a core factor in the therapeutic process but not the only factor. Healing often requires time and patience. It may necessitate a combination of counseling, medication, changes in environments and relationships, and treatments of organic or physical problems in the Identified Person that may call for referrals to other practitioners, i.e., medical doctors or psychiatrists, especially if a participant is suicidal or requires medical management of a chemical, biological, or hereditary diseases or disorders.

Interactional faith-based family practitioners use techniques to address most of these needs during treatment. However, even those licensed to do so often hesitate to use medication in therapy for several reasons:

1. Medications often mask symptoms and/or numb individuals to any recognized need for resolution of their problems by controlling any pain or discomfort that would otherwise encourage them to engage in the healing process and those activities involving paradigm shifts in underlying assumptions and beliefs.

2. The use of medication is theoretically inconsistent with the position of intentional change; the individual does not process the problem but merely expresses it in a more acceptable way, often relying on

defense mechanisms to drive decision-making that may modify thinking and behavior temporarily.

3. Most medications have little or no effect on the overall outcome in a person's ability to amend faulty mental maps or adjust their dysfunctional behaviors, often resulting in complacent compliance instead of genuine change. However, they may influence one's ability to access and process information for accurate or effective decision making.

4. Depending on the medications used, they can have severe psychological and physiological side effects related to chemical restraint or addiction and organic changes.

When entering into counseling or therapy, a key deterrent is that people may eventually come to believe that the medication determines the outcome, not their own efforts or engagement in the process. Therefore, unless absolutely necessary, the interactional faith-based family practitioner avoids the use of medication in therapy. If necessary, practitioners work closely with the participant to ensure the medication is used correctly. They may also confer with the prescribing physician or advanced practice provider to safely monitor the participant's treatment and ability to contribute to the therapeutic tasks and activities while being managed medically.

Expectations for how to support pharmacologically-induced behavior change must be established at the beginning of the counseling and therapy process. Practitioners present any concerns, limitations, and challenges participants on medications may encounter during therapy while taking part in treatment protocols and activities, as well as potential variances in therapy outcomes. Otherwise, it may call into question a practitioner's ethics when dealing with what appears to be unresolvable problems.

Addressing the possible influence of medications on participant behaviors helps practitioners and participants assess unsuccessful outcomes more realistically. Ethical questions about the utility of medication for participants in family therapy are:

1. Why reduce behavior that has reinforcing potential within treatment until its relevancy can be determined?

2. Will the administration of medication restrict or mask the practitioner's opportunities to recognize the relevant interactions that initiated the problem and are necessary in developing effective treatment strategies?

3. Was any failure to effect change related to the medications the participant was taking?

4. Should the participant have been referred to another therapist or medical specialist who works with psychotherapy approaches combined with medical models of care, *i.e.*, a licensed psychiatrist?

The role of medication and its perceived influence on behavior varies widely among family practitioners. When appropriate, the interactional faith-based family therapist normally consults with a medical doctor or psychiatrist, who is more inclined to use a pharmacological approach to treatment. However, referring a family or individual to a physician for help because of a potential need for some types of medication (*e.g.*, for organic diseases or disorders or some psychological disorders) does not automatically terminate the therapeutic relationship with the interactional faith-based family practitioner or any other form of conjoint therapy.

The total family system is disrupted when the medical needs of an Identified Person are interposed on the issue wherein behavioral change is sought by the other family members. For example, a child diagnosed with Attention Deficit Hyperactivity Disorder (ADHD) is put on medication. Generally, the focus of the practitioner would then shift to the spousal relationship and their continuing interactions relative to the child's normal state of being.

Whenever medication is involved, the practitioner must adapt his or her perceptions of the presenting problem and the dysfunctional system. Participants on medication frequently experience a certain degree of stereotyping with a conjoining attachment of labels. For example, the "hyperactive child" or the "autistic child" who fails to respond to medication but might respond well to positive attention, discipline, and structure within a supportive family unit. Such stereotyping and labeling could severely limit the therapeutic approaches possible and mask or distort important information needed by the practitioner to plan, implement, and evaluate relevant interventions.

It sometimes seems easier to chemically control behaviors temporarily with medications than to work through the disruptive and painful behaviors—the resistance and multifaceted complications that evolve out of the myriad of concerns and issues participants present for therapy and resolution and restored relationships. Nevertheless, attempting to move towards real mental, emotional, and spiritual health without those chemical controls calls for competent and dedicated family therapy practitioners working with equally engaged participants.

Healing of broken mental maps and dysfunctional behaviors demands genuine faith, determination, and a commitment to the therapeutic process by practitioners and participants alike. When everyone works together in this way, treatment does not usually take years to achieve successful outcomes.

PSYCHOMETRIC TESTS

Practitioners using traditional psychotherapies frequently assess their participants in therapy using *standard psychometric tests* (*e.g.*, Minnesota Multiphasic Personality Inventory, MMPI; or the California Personality Inventory, CPI). These tests are used to measure mental capabilities, personality traits, attitudes, and behavioral patterns. The results are often used to plan treatment approaches and therapeutic interventions based on the individual deficit model or medical model perspective.

However, interactional faith-based family therapy practitioners may also use such tests for collecting baseline information to help with diagnosing problems but see little or no value in using them for treatment. Realistically, all relevant information needed for any type of therapy is effectively obtained through subjective interviews. Some practitioners have suggested giving these tests when the deficit or dysfunction is presented as an intrapersonal problem. A diagnosis is part of the assessment and is an educational component of treatment, providing a starting point or place to begin therapy.

Current research and practice continue to update and modify psychometric tests based on scientific analysis of new data to be more accurate and relevant in diagnosing mental and behavioral problems than in the past. Yet the real value of these tests lies in their ability to provide a tangible form of perceived validation for decision-making in legal and psychological communities. When psychometric instruments are used, they should measure family dynamics and interactions at the level of relationship rather than just at the level of individuality.

LENGTH OF TREATMENT

Interactional Faith-Based Family Therapy differs from most psychodynamic therapies (*psychotherapy*) in that it is always short-term rather than comprehensive or long-term. A prolific amount of related literature has been written about both short-term and long-term theories of therapy. Findings presented in literature and practice continue to demonstrate how short-term therapeutic approaches have been more effective and less costly than long-term therapeutic approaches. This is particularly critical when working with families. Their ability to participate in numerous therapy sessions and related activities over a protracted period of time can limit how much of their personal and familial resources they can invest in the process.

It is important to note, though, that neither counseling nor therapy can be considered the same as mentoring, coaching, preceptoring, or personal training. Both counseling and therapy by their very natures are of limited durations. Termination of the therapeutic relationship is the goal for many psychotherapies, including counseling and interactional faith-based family therapy. Mentoring, coaching, and preceptoring can be intermittent and ongoing processes of indeterminate duration. At points of transition, practitioners may introduce activities for participants that include some coaching or mentoring as techniques for moving the therapy forward. Swihart and Figueroa (2014) describe the process techniques of coaching, mentoring, and preceptoring, tools that can enhance interactive faith-based family therapy.

Coaching is generally time-limited and relies on proximity. Parents may be asked to coach their children on how to perform the tasks assigned by the practitioner. Children may coach their parents in using new technology.

Mentoring does not rely on proximity and may continue for an indeterminant amount of time, *e.g.*, familial mentorships may last a lifetime. This process reflects the philosophy, faith and beliefs, culture, and relationships within the family unit. Children may ask a parent or grandparent to mentor them in learning about their ancestry. Parents may mentor children in how to learn from their failures as they grow and develop through debate, active listening, and open communication with one another.

Preceptoring is similar to interactive therapy. It is generally time-limited and combines the processes of coaching and mentoring to complete assigned tasks and achieve specific goals. Expectations and the boundaries of the relationship are established at the beginning of the process. Roles of participants are clearly defined. Negotiation of tasks and frequent feedback occur throughout the process. Practitioners work with participants to assess the presenting problem and its context, consider their needs and goals, set expectations, and plan the therapeutic tasks.

Correspondingly, interactional faith-based family therapy is of short duration. Treatment generally requires between 5 to 10 sessions. Effective changes reported and observed by the practitioner in individual (*i.e.,* the Identified Person) and family members related to improvements in problematic behaviors, faulty mental maps, and dysfunctional relationships indicate expectations and goals may have been met. This, then, would determine the time to terminate therapy.

However, while optimal therapy can occur over a short term with all family members present, the practitioner will need to work with abused persons and victims of abuse separately and possibly for a more extended period of time for positive change to occur. It is important to prevent family members from filtering and reinforcing negative or abusive behaviors or communication patterns while in session. In such a situation, the goal of interactional faith-based family therapy would be to eventually bring the family members back together and re-establish the family unit once effective individual changes have occurred in the Identified Person dealing with the real or perceived abuse.

REFRAMING, STORYTELLING, AND INTERPRETATION

The ahistorical (process) approach of interactional faith-based family therapy is not concerned with past events. It is developed basically through reframing of current situations and events. Practitioners address the presenting problems or dysfunctional behaviors and pose alternative perspectives that differ from the one individuals or families brought into therapy, *reframing* the event, situation, or circumstances. Simply put, the presenting problem might be accurate, but the practitioner may offer a side or aspect of it seemingly concealed or unseen by those involved.

Narrative therapy, a method of separating people from their problems and encouraging them to rely on themselves and their own problem-solving skills to minimize their impact. They do this through storytelling to connect with their experiences and to interpret their responses based on the stories they tell themselves grounded in three main ideas: (a) respect; (b) non-blaming; and, (c) views the client [participant] as the expert with the ability to change behavior and address issues (Ackerman, 2019).

Stories help people organize and mentally map their thoughts to give meaning and purpose to confusing events and broken relationships. A storytelling approach offers opportunities for individuals and families to revise or rewrite a story (re-author or re-story) to make it more acceptable to participants for managing stressful situations caused by past events.

Reframing works in a similar way to fold a dysfunctional narrative into the current situation to assess current mental maps and to present behaviors individually and within the family unit and how they can be reformed to change behaviors and heal relationships. Three elements are important to a positively reframed perspective. The reframing process:

1. Removes any tendency toward viewing an individual, *i.e.*, IP, as possessing an exploitable deficit;

2. Looks at all dysfunction within the individual and family unit at the systems level; and,

3. Considers a different perspective that is amenable to treatment by the practitioner.

Case studies are included in this book to serve as stories of processes or events that are analyzed to clarify or illustrate a perspective, concept, principle, or decision. In reviewing records of care or treatments that have helped others in similar situations, it becomes easier to see possible solutions or changes practitioners might implement to help guide participants through their current difficulties. Although a common problem with case studies is that they are limited in what they observe, identify, or target as important, or what they find to reconcile with an underlying bias of a practitioner or participant, they are a helpful tool in teaching and therapy. For example, faith-based family practitioners attempt to get beyond some of these limitations by guiding participants deeper into their mental maps and beliefs to help them see alternate possibilities and solutions. Let's look at a case study where interpretation and reframing inform the therapeutic approach.

CASE STUDY:
Interpretation and reframing

JD was an attractive, well-groomed 24-year-old woman described her presenting problem as *"I can't get close to people."* She stated that her childhood was a happy one. She had loving parents and a sister she liked as a sister. Her family members were devout members of a fundamental Protestant church. Most of JD's activities were church related. She had many friends during her childhood with one close girlfriend while in early adolescence. JD thought that her fear of closeness began when she slept over at her friend's house. During the night her friend began to fondle her in a way that JD *interpreted* as sexual. She became very frightened and felt guilty about this. She did not tell her parents because of her guilt and, in fact, had told no one before entering therapy. Although she attended college, she never dated and would participate only in superficial social contacts. She realized that this was not healthy young adult behavior and, as the behavior continued into her 20s, JD decided that she needed to seek help.

Assessment: Perhaps her need for a close relationship with her family was unavailable at the time of the incident. If her family was not there for her then, what she assumed to be sexual may have really been social, in that it appeared to fulfill a relational need that continued into her college years. If interactions with family and friends have more clearly defined roles, then it is safe to say that same-sex encounters would not hold one to predisposed or pre-determined lifestyles that may be unwanted. Therefore, the practitioner performed a cooperative *reframe* that changed JD's mental map around the incident, her role in the family structure, and her behavior in response to her perceived or lingering guilt.

The key element of reframing is that it gives the practitioner an opportunity to negotiate for change. The reframe is causal in that it removes blame, involves multiple people, and is ultimately solvable. Social needs are not sexual needs and same-sex encounters are not necessarily indicators of cultural identity or preference.

Usually, when the interactional faith-based family practitioner reframes, the family struggles to retain some of their original positions on their presenting problem and many times personal interpretations of selected beliefs are used to support the dysfunction. Two points should be emphasized when reframing:

1. Reframes involve subtle negotiation of perspective, followed by agreement, which contains a presenting problem amenable to treatment.

2. The flexibility to offer a solution to the assumed dysfunction can only be functional if the basics of common grace (forgiveness) are major components of a faith-based approach.

Interpretations generally reflect the practitioner's personal, subjective conception of the unconscious meaning of certain behaviors or utterances. Root causation is unilaterally determined without benefit of negotiation. A common feature of interpretations and the most powerful characteristic that differentiate an interpretation from a reframe is that *interpretation* is presented as correct and factually based without benefit of negotiation. A *reframe*, however, is not directive nor singularly confrontational but interactional and fluid between practitioner and participant.

Interestingly, when the participant disagrees with the historical interpretations of the practitioner, the participant may be labeled as resistant, hostile or perceived as lacking insight regardless of the circumstances or situation. The practitioner is assumed to be correct—the participant carries the deficit. However, a reframe of the presenting problem can provide an opportunity for negotiation to change or alter family structure and the participant is free to change the behavior.

IN CONCLUSION

While the focus in interactional faith-based family therapy is inclusive of individual faith and the family's dynamics, it is specific to the movement of family growth and the interactional relational processes. There may or may not be a focus in the family. Life is not stagnant—families are constantly in non-static, fluid, dynamic movement towards health or illness.

The role of the interactional faith-based family practitioner is to negotiate family relationships and beliefs towards necessary behavior and lowering levels of anxiety that result in improving the functionality of the family unit. The goal is to facilitate participants' ability to grow and prosper with or without the structure as an individual or member of a family unit. The family becomes the healthy relational system it was meant to be.

Working as an interactional faith-based family practitioner without a theory is like trying to teach faith without a theology. The practitioner often reduces obvious barriers but may be limited at certain times when the artisan's skill or the value, strength and durability of a changed life because of faith is not visible.

The background information in this chapter simply identifies some of the models used to change peoples' lives through some of the psychotherapies practiced today. Some are more effective for the short-term. However, they all employ methods and therapeutic techniques using various interactional tools to facilitate changes in problematic participant behaviors, flawed mental maps, and damaged relationships. These models are examples of humanity's attempts to resolve problems without tapping into the faith of participants. Therein lays their value—and their weakness.

Most of us would like a simple, humanistic prescription for our problems but quickly become confused and resistant when the symptoms do not respond to the prescribed therapeutic solution. It was not designed to do so. Biases must be set aside once the unknown is identified and faith becomes a part of the process. When faith is included in treating the whole person and family system, all the potential for genuine change becomes available to the practitioner and participants. At that point, the participant has the full force of efforts from every possible source of strength and healing.

CHAPTER 3:
Therapists and Theories

*Let no one presume to give advice to others that has not
first given good advice to himself.* -Seneca

Frequently lost among the concepts, techniques, and tasks of family counseling and therapy are the roles and theories unique to the faith-based
therapist, or practitioner. Practitioners elicit information from strangers,
alter their perspectives of a problem, and create changes in family interactional patterns of behavior that reflect their accepting of support and
healthy growth individually and as a family unit.

The therapeutic emphasis and work remain with both the practitioner and the family. Families are encouraged to implement changes recommended by the practitioner that reflect the quality of faith-based therapy
where faith is a factor. When it occurs, *resistance to change* often represents
inaccurate or inadequate conceptualizations of the problem, faulty mental
maps related to faith and its role in therapy, or inappropriate and unimag-
inative task assignments. Practitioners may encounter such resistance, for
example, when they fail to recognize or acknowledge the role of faith for
the individuals and their family units.

Ultimately, responsibility for genuine change belongs to the family
members individually and as a unit, or system. The practitioner inculcates

the reality of that responsibility into the therapy. If the family does not change, the practitioner may not have provided sufficient encouragement or opportunity for change to take place. Dysfunctional behaviors frequently act as defense mechanisms protecting familial relationships that deviate from what is considered normal by society or by the presenting family. Effective faith-based family practitioners engage in varied roles using multiple strategies to identify problematic patterns and counter the family's disruptive behaviors, employing their faith as an incentive for real and sustainable change.

PRACTITIONER ROLES

The interactional faith-based family practitioner's three primary roles represent specific spheres of practice: (1) healer, (2) artist, and (3) mental health professional. Each role involves a different set of skills, responsibilities, and benefits, depending on the therapy process and the expectations of the participants. Practitioners generally move seamlessly from one role to another as needed throughout the therapeutic process.

Role 1: Healer

In today's complex environments of healthcare, physicians treat physical disorders and, assuming a legitimacy of mind/body duality, others—usually psychotherapists—treat the mind. Psychiatrists are physicians who specialize in treating both body and mind. Biological **psychiatry** or *biopsychiatry*, a branch of medicine in **psychiatry** treating mental disorders by studying the **biological** function of the nervous system and seeking biomarkers for disease rather than treating clusters of signs and symptoms of non-organic mental illnesses, such as PTSD (post-traumatic stress disorder). Psychiatry, biopsychiatry, and most psychotherapies have effectively left a spiritual vacuum many practitioners attempt to fill using only physical and cognitive theories and techniques that are too often weak, ineffective, and lacking any significant healing ability.

Participants may present with physical disorders manifesting mental or emotional symptoms, thereby exposing how complicated therapy can become when working with individuals and families. For example,

- Fear of rejection or failure may be internalized as a body condition (*e.g.*, pain or fatigue)
- Spiritual distress may precipitate a life-threatening or suicidal response

When I declared not my sin, my body wasted away through my groaning all day long. For day and night thy hand was heavy upon me; my strength was dried up as by the heat of summer. -Psalm 32.3-4

Depression, malnutrition, and dehydration—until the psalmist's basic spiritual need to repent and be forgiven was met, no medicines or psychiatric treatments would be sufficient to bring complete healing. Meeting physical needs alone is not enough.

It is critical that practitioners recognize the basic or presenting problem bringing a family to therapy is not always obvious or singular. There cannot be genuine healing without considering the whole person when working with participants in the family system. Shelly, John, and others (1983) noted how diet, exercise, drugs (*e.g.*, alcohol, tobacco, prescription medications), and general health affect how people think, feel, and make decisions. Relationships help shape concepts of self and others, goals, values, and approaches life and well-being. Education and life experiences form life and world views, mental maps, and influence behavior. Spiritually, a relationship with God gives "ultimate meaning and purpose to life, a basic sense of security and belonging, and the ability to love and forgive. An unhealthy relationship with God can create serious physical and emotional disorders" (p. 26).

The role of healer requires practitioners to consider all dimensions of being when working with families: physical, mental, and spiritual. Practitioners working within accepted ethical parameters and standards of practice have the unique ability, power, and insight to say or do nearly anything in therapy needed to facilitate behavior changes and help participants realign their mental maps. They do this with authority and influence, or *presence*. As healers, practitioners demonstrate presence in session, for example, when they project subtle confidence as they structure and manage therapy sessions. By determining what occurs in therapy, how and when it occurs, the practitioner brings to the session the presence needed to assess and guide new patterns for the possibility for change to occur.

Role 2. Artisan

In the role of artisan, effective interactional faith-based family practitioners engage in the *art* of therapy. They function along a continuum as sales people and thespians. The practitioner often commands attention through drama, always presenting interactive methods directly or indirectly. Faith-based practitioners are constantly working with moving targets, *i.e.*, when the therapist sets expectations for sessions—some task or activity—to confront dysfunctional behaviors, for example, only to find when it is met or resisted, the target moves to yet another problematic expectation, behavior, or mental map. They recognize that for people of faith, God is the only One with the clarity to fix those moving targets to facilitate genuine or lasting change.

In the role of artisan, practitioners have the ability to determine and modify the process of change as it occurs. There is nothing noble about completing a directive, task, or activity if subsequent failure is evident. Practitioners initiate processes to help participants win and not lose opportunities to change. Like a craftsman working in a complex and ever-shifting medium, practitioners strive to create therapeutic activities that embody faith, simplicity, parsimony, and integrity, always respecting the beliefs of participants. These exercises should not be overtly obvious or presumptive but take the therapy to the next level for change to occur. The goal is to develop a clear picture without the participant's problems obscuring the change issue. Practitioners are concerned with the art of subtle influence, facilitating changes in patterns of interactions and behaviors so that healthy self-confidence can surface and new ways of engaging in relationships can emerge and grow.

Role 3. Mental health professional

Mental health is a complicated, imprecise, and value-laden term, difficult to define beyond pertaining to psychological, emotional, and social well-being, affecting how people think, feel, and act. Interactional faith-based family practitioners often serve in the role of mental health professional, though some practitioners with additional education and experience may also be specialists in psychology. Shelly, John, and others (1983) describe mental health from a faith perspective as "a state of dynamic equilibrium characterized by hope, joy and peace, in which positive self-regard is developed through the love, relationship, forgiveness, meaning and purpose resulting from a vital relationship with God and a responsible interdependence with others" (p. 27).

Regardless of level of expertise, practitioners must possess knowledge and wisdom about human behavior and relationships. They strive to reduce the false information and myths about families and relational interactions. Then, faith-based family therapists typically move to assist families in normalizing their presenting problems, which helps them establish a dynamic equilibrium wherein there may be frequent ups and downs but overall a steady state is maintained. Families in this state of balance between continuing and variable processes are usually more flexible in their decision-making, able to cope with stress and crises related to dysfunctional behaviors and faulty mental maps, adjust to change, resolve problems and conflicts among participants within the family unit.

Mental health is a complex variable that comprises a wide range of emotional, mental, and behavioral processes of an individual in relationship to God, self, and others. Paul Meehl, a psychologist, asserted, "If man were in the proper relationship to God, he would not feel condemned (either by God, his fellows, or himself); he would derive the richest, truest, and most satisfying meanings, because in all things he would be God-oriented" (1958, p. 216). Mentally healthy families give and receive love and forgiveness, confront one another, give and receive constructive criticism, and express anger safely and respectfully, affirm one another, and are grounded in interactive faith-based relationships that provide the stability needed to enable them to risk addressing dysfunctional behaviors and faulty mental maps to facilitate individual and relational change and growth. The value of an individual or family before God is not dependent on mental or physical health. In faith-based family therapy, participants come to recognize that every human being—every member of the family unit—shares the spiritual need for meaning and purpose, for love and connectedness, and for forgiveness and hope.

Interactional faith-based practitioners encounter many approaches and techniques used by psychotherapists and counselors. Libraries are filled with the latest "pop" (i.e., popular) psychology books with ideas and activities to work with individuals and families through counseling and therapy. The many complex and unique problems families contend with demand active interventions call for practitioners to be familiar with the various trends in mental health (e.g., inner child or co-dependency) and psychotherapies. It is imperative that interactional faith-based family practitioners stay current in following scientific literature and continue advancing their own professional growth in their specialty practices and skills in family therapy. These resources provide practitioners with additional perspectives and research for working with individuals and families of diverse faith backgrounds and religious traditions (Carson & Koenig, 2008).

PRACTITIONER SKILLS

The authors have observed that often families seem to prefer to sit and talk to ordinary people trained in the mechanics of psychotherapy because responses depend on well-rehearsed cues or prescribed formats that never change (*e.g.*, "Tell me more..."; or "...and how do you feel about that?"). However, this scripted method does not enhance therapy any more than rote prayers enhance worship. Skills in natural social interactions generally serve the practitioner much more efficiently in accurately asking questions (*e.g.*, "If were to change their behaviors, would that cause you to behave differently towards them? If so, what would you want them to change, and how would you respond to those changes?").

Effective interactional faith-based family practitioners have the expertise to direct the therapy process during normal, interactive conversations in session. At their core, practitioners' skills rest in an ability to alter the perspective of the family, shifting the process from an *individual deficit model* to an *interpersonal model* through collaborative negotiations. Practitioners determine what the family members believe about the presenting problems and what they need to believe to change behaviors and realign their mental maps.

When the family can reframe the presenting problem so that it becomes interactional, relational, and correctable, the problem ceases to be irrational or entrenched in the IP or family system. In Structural Family Therapy (1981, 2014), Minuchin directs the family to view their problem as a malleable entity that is distinct and independent of the IP or family unit. He then uses his therapeutic skills to remold that entity.

1. First, he joins the family, building a coalition with them.

2. Minuchin then modifies or alters the relationships within the family. *Modification* occurs when one participant states the position needed and the family accepts it.

3. If they disagree, the therapist backs up, agrees that their perspective is possible, and then offers an alternate possibility that is slightly different than the one initially offered.

4. This process continues until the dysfunctional patterns become healthy patterns.

As practitioners develop greater negotiation skills, they increasingly recognize the appropriate times to agree and disagree with participants. In a sense, interactional faith-based family therapists are a type of engineer consulting on ongoing projects for which the original blueprints were lost. They hold the necessary equipment and must, therefore, take some responsibility if legitimate attempts to repair the problems fail.

PRACTICE PITFALLS

Practitioners must never argue with participants or confront them as some psychotherapists recommend. The objective is to change behavior patterns and perspectives rather than attitudes, which is best served by clergy or spiritual advisors. When individuals describe a belief or myth that is incompatible with the approaches the practitioner wants to take with the family—do not oppose them. When faith-based family therapists engage in conflict with the participants, they lose their therapeutic power and leverage for facilitating change and healing.

A gentle answer turns away wrath, But a harsh word stirs u anger. The tongue of the wise makes knowledge acceptable. But the mouth of fools spouts folly. -Proverbs 15.1-2

Unmanaged conflict can be a major pitfall to progress. When confrontations occur, the session usually ceases to be either therapeutic or safe. The only redeeming advantage arises if the conflict becomes a controlled intervention. Otherwise, no further work can be accomplished in a now hostile setting until the conflict is resolved or redirected to more appropriate interactions. Ultimately, though, there will be no further compliance by the family members under any circumstances without the leverage and authority of a practitioner in control of the emotional environment and the behaviors of those present.

Sometimes a practitioner contaminates the session by bringing in other psychotherapeutic approaches, techniques, or experiences that are not a part of the interactional faith-based family therapy model. All practitioners are guilty of bringing in that which has been comfortable—but not necessarily effective—from past training or previous experiences in therapy or counseling. The disconnects in approaches or techniques distract the participants and move the practitioner into other modalities that have attached themselves to family therapies over the years. Consequently, such a potpourri of theories and techniques interfere with planning and goal setting by confusing them with the interactional faith-based family therapy approach. For example, when practitioners use a psychodynamic approach, they may stumble into the pitfall of shifting from an interpersonal model back to an individual deficit model. At that point, they are no longer doing interactional family therapy.

THEORY DETERMINES TECHNIQUE

Any theory, hypothesis, sect, philosophy, creed or institution, that fears investigation, openly manifests its own error. -Andrew Jackson Davis

A *theory* is the formulation of underlying principles of observed phenomena related to a specific area of interest that has been verified to some degree. It gathers information and sets the direction of change. For example, the theory of the family as a system describes how one might think about family functioning and change. In family therapy, theory is formulated first and defines the questions needed to facilitate change within the family first.

Theory determines technique, which confirms the objectives of the therapy. Technique acts as the vehicle for the questions defined by theory. *Technique* in interactional family therapy functions like a composite of ahistorical models, attempting to resolve specific problems through interactional activities and tasks. Conversely, if technique preceded theory, then more counseling would occur than therapy. For example, getting people to express themselves in session does not necessarily support family therapy or affirm family hierarchy or boundaries.

Presenting problems

The *presenting problem* is usually the reason for the initial contact for therapy or counseling. The one assumption made regarding the presenting problem is that there is some interactional dysfunction being reflected. All interventions are designed to allow the behavior to change by providing alternative behavior patterns or a new perspective on the existing pattern by aligning mental maps of the family dynamics within the system.

If the problem is long standing, practitioners may assume it has purpose in feeding behavior or relational dysfunction, much like ineffective but protective defense mechanisms. Therefore, to perpetuate a maladaptive system, the presenting problem allows some members of the family unit to meet or even exceed their own perceived expectations of normalcy.

The best way to detect the perceived impact of the presenting problem is to ask the question, "What occurs as a result of the presenting problem?" A seemingly simple question, it calls forth an entire range of behavior and emotional responses when the consequences of the question are recognized. Theory dictates that the following areas be directly or indirectly addressed:

1. Does the presenting problem change the likelihood of any other behavior? Or...

2. Increase interaction with family members? Or...

3. Incite antagonism with one another?

Perspective of theory

In effect, theory determines what is relevant and what is not. Theory attends to only those aspects of interaction that alter patterns of behavior and are pertinent to the situation or needs of the family unit. The construction of questions in therapy shapes the therapy process and continuously changes the information available to the practitioner. The perspective of theory (*i.e.*, the Family Therapy Approach) occurs when the information comes from both internal changes and external changes (what occurs between and among persons).

Questions are tools defined by theory, not techniques. The type of questions used reveals the practitioner's theory of therapy. A combination of the questions in the interactional family therapist's toolkit provides a key resource for stimulating effective change: power questions, clarification questions, transition questions, and change questions. (See Table 3.1.)

Table 3.1. Questions to guide change		
Type	**Purpose**	**Examples**
Power questions	Enable the practitioner to maintain control and direct the session	What is gained by the presenting problem? Who gains by the presenting problem? What are the consequences of the presenting problem? What is the function of the presenting problem? Why does the presenting problem occur now?
Clarification questions	Enable the therapist to identify, define and validate the presenting problem	How is the presenting problem defined? —by actual behavior? —by family agreement? —by family or personal myth? Who confirms the defined problem? —by other families? —by the media? —by medication usage? —by mental health workers?

Transition questions	Enable the therapist to reframe the presenting problem	What makes the behavior a problem? —the behavior itself? —the timing? —the consequences? For whom is it a problem? —for other family members? —for school? for friends? for work?
Change questions	Enable the therapist to secure the changed behavior	What patterns need to be altered? Who needs to be present? What family structural changes are needed? —joining subunits (mother and father, child with peers) —dividing units into subunits. (separate parent and child, form therapist coalition with each) —therapeutic leverage (who gains by not viewing behavior as a problem?) Who gains by the most change, by the least change, or with no change? (who can help the therapist?)

Perspective of technique

If theory determines technique, then techniques are subject to therapeutic maneuvers initiated by practitioners. *Therapeutic maneuvers*, such as reframing or relabeling, are typical in many therapeutic approaches. Any subsequent reduction in the presenting problem following the use of a technique implies indirect support for a specific theory.

As a technique is implemented, in-session (*e.g.*, reframe or enactment) or out-of-session (*e.g.*, strategic tasks), the responses by family members provide information about relevant interactional patterns of behavior and mental maps. Questions with family members, for example, that cast doubt on a current family strategy for handling a particular situation or behavior, provide alternate patterns for investigation.

All techniques generate data for the practitioner to examine and use to probe the patterns in the family unit or in each individual member's contextual framework. Techniques allow the practitioner an opportunity to assess structure within the family system. Structural techniques such as *enactment* (*i.e.*, having a couple talk to each other or other members of the family) generate relevant information and are considered in-session interactions. The practitioner might note:

1. Who answers and in what order?

2. How do they answer?

3. What nonverbal cues are given?

Each separate data point is meaningless. When a sequence redundancy is observed, the practitioner can hypothesize that the pattern is meaningful (*e.g.*, a woman speaks glowingly about her husband's virtues yet frequently mentions her concerns about her role as wife; her nonverbal cues and sequence redundancy about personal inadequacy support a meaningful pattern of behavior).

Some techniques, especially strategic tasks, generate out-of-session responses. Specifically, interactive family practitioners question what sequences occurred that allowed the task to be completed, not completed, or halfway completed. They are observing patterns on at least two levels: (a) presenting problems and (b) response to techniques. *Response to technique* determines the next therapeutic move because, in family therapy, response to technique is response to treatment.

Structure and pattern in family therapy

There is a difference between structure and pattern. *Structure* determines pattern. *Pattern* refers to sequence of behavior. Structure is the arrangement of roles and responsibilities in response to pre-established beliefs. Therefore, to the individual, structure refers to the arrangement of roles and responsibilities within his or her context of life. The following axioms help in correctly viewing patterns and structure:

1. *Structure* determines the pattern

2. *Pattern* reflects structure

3. See the pattern and assume the structure

4. *Structure* is the skeleton; *pattern* is the skin

Most family therapy techniques are intended to change the patterns generating or supporting the presenting problem. Technique is the level where the practitioner enters into the family's dysfunctional patterns. This point is usually behavioral but could be cognitive, although cognitive patterns (*i.e.*, mental maps) are normally at the myths or beliefs level. If the point of entry is behavioral, practitioners may assign a task to provide opportunity for a changed pattern. If the point of entry is cognitive, change structure to provide opportunity for a changed pattern.

An example of how practitioners might assess the structure of the family during a session might be seen when a father consistently looks at the mother to correct the behavior of a young child during the session. The father's role would be to supervise parenting—from a distance. If the mother complies and corrects the child's behavior, the practitioner can assume that the mother's role is to keep the child's behavior respectable in public. No questions need be asked about the roles they play.

Role of the participant in family therapy

The parental unit is considered the primary source of control and influence for children. To the interactional faith-based family practitioner, the parental unit is also designed for protection and nurturing. This carries two implications: (a) if the parents provide poor models for behavior, the children will show adjustment problems; and, (b) change in children's behavior always necessitates therapy beginning with the parents. Children tend to normalize families. Therapy models approach the parental role of the participant differently. (See Table 3.2.)

Table 3.2. Therapy models and parental roles	
Family Therapy Model	**Description**
Structural Family Therapy	Views the parents as occupying the top level of the hierarchy; there is a need for boundaries and subsystem interventions to set alternate boundaries; therapy issues involve values
Strategic Family Therapy	Similar to Structural Therapy but with the emphasis on power; parents should exercise appropriate power over children from the top of the hierarchy; therapy issues involve authority
Behavioral Family Therapy	Puts the emphasis on parental skills; assumes poor parenting for a number of reasons that impede the expression the skills; therapy issues involve responsible leadership
Multigenerational Family Therapy	Holds that parent failure is due to unresolved issues with previous generations and individualization, which create marital conflict and aberrant behavior because of triangle conflict; therapy issues involve inherited or learned implications

Interactional faith-based family therapists are more likely to choose one of the above approaches to identify presenting problems. This enables the practitioner to identify structural and pattern dysfunctions, to select preferred techniques, and to begin the therapeutic process. It is understood in family therapy that everyone is a parent, has a parent, or will become a parent. The familial interaction—whether realized or presupposed—is the basis for therapy.

Relationship is basic to interactive family therapy. Therefore, treatment is not focused on an identified person (IP), but rather on what occurs between or among individual members of the family unit. Accepting a faith-based position in life is the responsibility of the individual. Problem often arise when one family member is a person of faith and another is not. The fact of the dysfunctional relationship, then, becomes the question of faith.

IN CONCLUSION

If therapy is an art, then theory only dictates how the interactional faith-based family practitioner thinks about behavior and therapy while engaging in the various roles needed throughout the process to bring about healing and change. Technique is what they do in response to their theories. Practitioners can know all the theories and every technique possible and still be ineffective. Timing and rationale are more important than expressing positive regard, moving chairs, or producing paradoxes or counter-paradoxes during in-session interactions.

To a mature practitioner, theory—and not technique—determines the approach to family therapy. Techniques are not a set of behavioral acts independent of context, but rather as the behavioral extensions of the theory. The practitioner's techniques evolve during therapy as a way of thinking and may be driven with and through the vehicle of questions. For example, the structural technique of enactment is expressed in the format of interactional questions in-session, such as "What nonverbal cues are given by each family member present?" In the next chapter, we will dive deeper into the function of interactional questions and how they can be used to bring about change.

CHAPTER 4:
Function of Interactional Questions

The most important thing in communication is to hear what isn't being said.
-John W. Roper

Communication, the giving or interchanging of thoughts, feelings, and information occurs through a combination of verbal and nonverbal responses via indirect or casual transmission. Questioning is done to obtain information, start conversations, teste and confirm understanding, explore possibilities, draws participants into critical thinking activities, *e.g.*, engaging in reasoning exercises, building confidence, and seeking support or agreement. (Tanzi, 2015)

Interactional questions form the basis of effective family therapy and act as a key to accurate communication with participants. Appropriate questions reveal underlying mental maps guiding behaviors, alter perspectives, and facilitate change by provoking and gently probing family relationships by challenging them without direct confrontation.

This activity can indirectly foster access to the family's belief system, an important part of the process when providing interactional faith-based family therapy. This type of questions has four primary functions:

1. Reflect the practitioner's perspective;

2. Request change in an interactional manner;

3. Alter participant perspectives; and,

4. Introduce more possibilities for change.

The structural technique of enactment expressed within the context of these questions in-session draws on participants' verbal and nonverbal cues. The practitioner monitors the behaviors and responses of each of the family members as the questions are being considered by the participants.

INTERACTIONAL PERSPECTIVES

Interactional perspective arises from questions the practitioner asks when an individual's thinking becomes interactional. The phrasing of the question allows the therapist to receive information without developing mental barriers to what is being presented by participants. It acts as a safe rationale for reviewing presenting problems. The interactional perspective implies the participant, usually the IP, can manage those problems. Family members may recognize reflective responses as new perspectives with elements of control and hope.

The interactional perspective develops when the faith-based family practitioner uses interactional questions to transition the process from merely gathering general information to initiating change while requesting information for that change. This approach is more effective when the practitioner works with at least two or more family members or persons.

The practitioner's request for information needed to facilitate change is presented in question form and usually occurs outside of any specific task:

1. What might be a different response if you believed things could change the way you act now?

2. If you did it differently, do you believe such a change would cause the other person to change, as well?

The practitioner alters the participant perspective by redefining, reframing, or re-representing the problem. This is done by assigning another role in the dysfunctional pattern, but without an assumed individual deficit attached. The questions are asked in a manner to guide the interactions, so the family can adopt the restructured thinking as their own, thereby beginning the process of changing those mental maps linked to the presenting problem: "Do you think this might have been understood differently had you known the entire story?"

STORY: Guiding perspective by shifting the paradigm

A frazzled man with several noisy children entered a crowded bus. The man took no notice of the energetic playfulness of his children nor of the disturbance they caused the other passengers. One particularly irritated woman decided to take the negligent and seemingly uncaring man to task. She boldly confronted him.

"I'm so sorry," the man humbly whispered, pulling the youngest child to him. "You see, my wife—their mother—died this morning and the children and I are feeling rather alone and frightened. I'm afraid that we haven't quite been able to take it all in just yet..."

A great sadness and ready compassion for the suffering of the small family immediately restructured the woman's thinking and her former irritation was quickly forgotten.

This simple story is an example of what is generally referred to as a *paradigm shift* in thinking and a basic spiritual approach to facilitating change in a faith-based family therapy practice.

BEHAVIOR CHANGE

In therapy, interactional questions function primarily to change the focus of participant behaviors and the mental maps guiding them. A second function of these questions serves to move the therapeutic focus from the general patterns to the specific behavior. To do this when behavior changes and perspectives shift, a few formal tasks are necessary to help participants change relevant patterns and enable therapy to occur.

Indirect requests for behavior changes are generally best. They do not need explicit reasons to accompany them. Frequently, direct requests for behavior changes only generate excuses about why the identified behaviors cannot be changed. Practitioner questions, then, might sound like:

1. I don't think that can occur. What about you?

2. Most people would avoid doing that and I can understand why. How about you?

Practitioners examine the behaviors and responses of participants while collecting information and guiding the questions and indirect requests. The nonverbal responses, *e.g.*, gestures, body language, posture, personal space, seating choices by family members in-session, all provide important data about the participants, their relationships, and their perspectives around the presenting problem behavior.

TYPES OF INTERACTIONAL QUESTIONS

The conscious application of questioning is critical to understanding the mental maps, behaviors, and relational processes participants use to interact with one another (Tanzi, 2015). Three types of interactional questions most frequently used in interactional faith-based family therapy include: informational questions; rhetorical questions; and, hyperboles.

Informational questions

Informational questions (sometimes referred to as *forensic interviewing*) have two goals: (a) to gather information, and (b) to shift the perspective away from the individual toward the context of the problem and the participant family interactions. Sample questions include:

1. With all that is going on at home, what other things are affected?

2. What gets worse when (the problem) occurs?

3. How does your behavior affect the problem?

In family therapy, the problem is usually not the identified person (IP), but rather involves the relational family dynamics of all participants. The practitioner does not disagree with those who select an IP in the family as a *scapegoat* (*i.e.*, the one chosen by family members to blame for the problems, errors, mistakes, or faults of others). Instead, the therapist asks questions to develop an interactional perspective and to acknowledge each family member's contributions to the presenting problem. The questions are formed in a manner that describes an agreed-upon resolution, *e.g.*, "What might have been different if this had been handled otherwise?" Here the interactional faith-based family practitioner might offer faith as part of an option that the IP (or scapegoat) might react differently if the behavior causing the problem was viewed or processed otherwise.

Generally, the practitioner avoids establishing the causation of the problem as resulting from something historical or predetermined by any past event. Reasons given for current dysfunctional behaviors or faulty mental maps are often simply excuses to not change a behavior or way of thinking. For example, in cases where parenting is lacking, it may seem easier to shift the blame to a historical drinking problem. While that may be a true fact, the drinking problem remains a separate issue to address at a different time. Otherwise, the incompetence of the parenting behaviors easily becomes buried in the drinking problem until the drinking problem is resolved. Meanwhile, the dysfunctional and incompetent parenting becomes more deeply embedded in the family's overall pattern of behavior.

The faith-based practitioner carries the responsibility to maintain the focus and direction of interactions in the therapy sessions. This is done by selectively choosing an individual issue and building a path towards healthy familial interactions based on the information gathered on that specific issue or problem presented. These activities, coupled with the data collected with the information questions, are necessary to increase the family's functional behavior potential and advance their faith it can be changed.

Rhetorical questions

Rhetorical questions are statements in question form that do not require an answer or verbal response. They are the "tent pegs" of therapy used for engaging participants and drawing them into agreeing with the practitioner's perspective. They anchor the session and hold the shape and size of it in place. Rhetorical questions do not state facts directly but help illustrate a shift in participant perspective. For example, the practitioner might ask:

1. How do you believe you might have heard what was said differently if you had spent more time with the person who said it?
2. Is there a better way of expressing what you believe was said?

Because the response is irrelevant, therapy occurs through the structuring of the question itself—and often without immediate recognition by the participant or family unit.

Hyperboles

Hyperboles are figures of speech that exaggerate or emphasize an idea or behavior to make a point. The hyperbole pushes the participants' thinking beyond the capabilities or desires of a set pattern as it manipulates mental maps—sometimes in a humorous way—to establish a more functional pattern:

1. How can you stand being together when you are so much alike?
2. Why don't you give up and send the children to reform school, so others can learn from them?

Practitioners use hyperbolic interactional questions that amplify a situation sometimes to make a less extreme standpoint more comfortable and acceptable to participants.

INTERACTION QUESTION FORMATS

The conscious and considered selection of questions and how they will be applied in therapy is critical to accurate and caring communication with participants. Interactional questions must be carefully measured before they are asked. They can have both immediate and long-range significance and consequence. The practitioner must think through the process by asking what information is needed and, what is the intended perspective shift.

1. *What is needed?* What information is necessary to make an informed decision about dysfunctional interactional patterns?

2. *What perspective shift is necessary?* At what point will the practitioner shift the perspective toward a solvable interpersonal dysfunction instead of towards an individual pathology?

The faith-based family therapist can then engage the entire family as a method of healing the identified dysfunctional patterns when equipped with enough information and a designated perspective, or paradigm, shift. If a family member refuses to participate in the therapeutic process, it is possible to extend those members present into that member's perspective of influence. For example, when a spouse is missing; but, one parent and the children are present in-session, the practitioner might ask: "How does your behavior with your children affect their behavior when you and your spouse disagree?"

REFERENCE FORMAT

An interactional question can be stretched to reference not only affective responses, but also behavioral responses and cognitive responses reflecting current mental maps. The affective reference format is considered by many practitioners, both counselors and therapists—to be the only effective tool for questioning participants. However, the behavioral and cognitive usage of questions further expand the potential positive outcomes of whole family therapy. *Reference formats* enable the practitioner to help the family eventually alter their dysfunctional patterns. Examples of reference format questions are:

1. Who else in your family believes the way you do?
2. What is the problem as you understand it?

The three basic types of interactional questions most commonly seen in reference format are: open questions, closed questions, and funnel questions (Tanzi, 2015).

Open question format

Open questions usually provoke longer, more thoughtful responses, often leading to further discussion and elaboration of ideas and concerns. They provide opportunities for self-expression and encourage critical thinking and reasoning as participants contribute to the conversation initiated or expanded by the question.

Just as the reference question format identifies presenting problems or dysfunctional patterns, the open question format explains what they are about. It is here that a cause-and-effect observation may be seen, but only to the extent that all family members join in the conversation to explore the problem. Questions generally occur in sequence:

1. When does he/she behave this way?

2. How do they know when to act that way?

3. How does their behavior change when you are there?

4. How does your response or behavior affect their behavior?

5. What do they need to believe for you to do less so they can change their behavior?

Closed question format

The use of *closed questions* is somewhat limited because they are so specific and directive. Generally, they can be answered in one or two words (*e.g.*, yes/no). Very little verbal information is collected but can help focus discussion and gain clear, concise answers when needed. The practitioner forms the answer within the question as it is asked. The purpose is to shift the participant's perspective. Rhetorical questions are frequently asked in a closed question format. For example, to solidify a position in marriage, one might ask: "Do you think that if the two of you could decide together how to be supportive of each other's needs, this would indicate an improvement in the relationship and the current behavior would immediately change?"

Practitioners may also use closed format questions to test understanding, close out a discussion or make a decision, set the frame of the interaction, or shut down a conversation. If used incorrectly, closed questions can eventuate in awkward or troubling silences or participant refusals to continue the conversation or interaction. They can end a session.

Funnel question format

Funnel questions usually start with closed questions and, as the practitioner progresses through the funnel, ask more open questions. They guide the flow of the questions, moving the problem from the general to the specific to gather more and more details. This format is often used to find out more detail about a specific behavior or issue. They also help practitioners gain the interest or increase the confidence of the participants being questioned.

Summarizing and closing

Before ending the session, the practitioner may give a brief review of the main points, concerns, or conclusions raised during the conversation around the questioning process. *Summarizing* encourages each participant to review and agree on the points discussed thus far and acts as a guide to move the familial relationships forward.

Interactional questions are therapeutic when asked using these different approaches, particularly when they are delivered to the whole family or directed to one member and heard by the others. At times the question may be directed to one member but be specific to another member. At other times, the family might be removed from the therapy room, all except for one member. The therapist must always assume the problem is interactional and nothing more, or risk contaminating interactional therapy with more traditional psychotherapies. When therapists take the time to summarize and *close* a session, they give participants an opportunity to come back together, to finish their thoughts or comments if needed, and to arrange for any tasks or activities to be completed before the next session.

INTERACTIONAL QUESTIONS TO AVOID

There are specifically two kinds of interactional questions that must be avoided at all times: redundant questions and empty questions.

Redundant questions

Redundant questions are often used during interrogations and may make a participant—or the family unit—feel threatened.

1. After a family member says that he or she *hates to be ignored* and the therapist says, "What does he or she do that bothers you?"
2. Someone states that they are upset and angry and the therapist says, "Why do you think you are angry and upset?"

Better-phrased, interactional questions would be:

1. What do you do to let (another person) know you are being ignored? Or,

2. How do you want (someone) to change his or her behavior so that you might avoid becoming angry?

Empty questions

Empty questions have little substance provided by the practitioner. They may indicate he or she is confused or uncertain of how to proceed with therapy. These questions are used extensively in traditional psychodynamic therapies where the focus is on an individual rather than a family unit. The process is more talk therapy, which may include little or no interaction otherwise.

1. How do you feel about that?

2. Could you tell me more about that?

A better interactional question would be: "Can you tell me how you will let (someone) know that what once happened successfully, will not work again?" This format question is similar to the format used in the Milan Systemic Family Therapy (Lebow, 2017).

IN CONCLUSION

Questions are powerful tools. Tanzi (2015, p.154) describes six important purposes for using interactive questions carefully and respectfully in faith-based family therapy:

1. *Learning*: use open and closed questions; probing questions

2. *Relationship building*: respectfully explore participants' ideas, opinions, fears, needs, expectations, and goals

3. *Managing and guiding*: rhetorical and leading questions help participants reflect and commit to goals, therapeutic activities, and targeted outcomes

4. *Avoiding misunderstandings*: probing questions for clarification

5. *Diffusing difficult or emotionally-charged situations*: funnel questions distract and focus participants as they consider more details about a situation, behavior, or issue and their concerns or beliefs related to it; help them find practical ways to deal with the emotion attached to the situation while seeking ways to address it rationally

6. *Persuading others*: open questions help participants embrace reasons—instead of excuses—behind the behaviors or accept the practitioner's perspective

Questions asked carelessly or thoughtlessly can hinder or shut down communication because participants may feel uncomfortable or even threatened. Practitioners must use skill and active listening to gain and facilitate mutual understanding when questioning participants. For example, they might reflect on how a participant responded to a question to clarify the content of their answer, such as exploring the meaning behind a participant's denial of "faith in anything" while attending church every week.

When asking questions about individual or familial beliefs and values, for example, faith is best explained relative to the steadfast trust of the family that the therapist has earned for him or her to ask sometimes deeply personal and directive questions safely. The family then has an opportunity to attach their thinking and responding with renewed faith in how they express themselves, giving the practitioner the information needed to help them work toward change.

For faith to be integrated into family practice respectfully and successfully, practitioners must recognize and understand the theology of therapy they follow and draw on for themselves, when formulating their questions and treatment plans, and when interacting with participants. People often hold different beliefs and express their faith in unique ways with their own traditions and values which may vary from those held by the practitioner. In the next chapter and before moving further into preparing a plan of therapy for participants, we will explore the concept of theology and how it relates to interactional faith-based family therapy.

CHAPTER 5:
Theology and Ethics in Therapy

It is a great mistake to suppose that God is interested only, or even primarily, in religion. -William Temple

The task of developing a theology in therapy including academia and most clergy has been virtually impossible without normal philosophical limitations and anomalies. Many attempts have been made to force psychology into an untenable position perceived to be superior or equal to theology. For the most part some practitioners of faith-based therapies erroneously decry psychology as a soft or non-genuine science—too secularized to be of any real value in working with families of faith because of faith not being considered a fact.

However, the best approach for the family therapist practioner is to view theology and psychology independently without negating or dismissing the validity of either discipline. There cannot be a successful stand-alone therapeutic approach or intervention using only one discipline or the other—psychology or theology. Neither can integration of the two disciplines help without blurring the processes of both disciplines and diminishing their potential effectiveness in faith-based family therapy. To be effective, faith-based family practitioners must concentrate on similarities of function. The similarities in function are not meant to be and are practically impossible to establish and articulate in both therapy and ethics.

Similarities *in* and *of* function—what's the difference?

Similarities IN *function* involve a universal striving for mental health. *Similarities* OF *function* encompass the specific function of (a) psychology, the ability to explain humanity's perception of itself, and (b) theology, the ability to explain God's perception of humanity and the need for His grace, forgiveness, and salvation. Theology and psychology need not compete with one another but may complement one another within the context of human beings reaching out to comfort one another. For example, Jesus repeatedly modeled this approach in his interactions with his apostles and all of those who followed them before academics recognized his intent and labeled the process as theology.

THEOLOGY IN THERAPY

The very best and utmost act of attainment in this life is to remain still and let God act and speak to thee. -Meister Eckhart

Theology is the study of God. *Psychology* is the study of the mind. Theology and psychology are best understood in the origins of life when coupled with the function of therapy. Theology explains the interactions of God's relationship with humanity. Psychology records dysfunctions and evaluates their impact on individuals and their families as they are exposed to their environment and their social and personal needs.

Faith-based practitioners can use the dysfunctional in finding the functional within individuals and family systems. This may be represented by a peace provided by God's grace and the clarity of communication or the need for support due to individual deficits or problems in a dysfunctional family system. The following tenets provide a basic introduction to a theology in therapy based upon a distinct, limitless perception of grace and faith (Figure 5.1). Practitioners of a faith-based interactional family systems approach:

1. Offer hope as an unearned gift

2. Create change through personal interventions using techniques and maneuvers

3. Identify the source of change as something other than chance

4. Encourage the identified person (IP) and family members to own the changes

5. Engage the IP and family members in recognizing their individual personal needs, expectations, and goals

6. Develop and implement a treatment plan that can be superseded by God

Figure 5.1: Tenets of a theology in doing therapy		
Tenet: Faith-based family practitioners:	Description of Transition	Support of Faith
1. **Offer hope as an unearned gift**	For faith to exist, the idea of hope must be given freely as well. Motivation to expend the energy needed to change comes from the passion that hope provides.	Faith, hope, love, but the greatest of these is Love. -I Corinthians 13.13
2. **Create change through personal interventions, using techniques and maneuvers**	An intervention is done to modify, settle, or hinder an action or behavior. In interactional faith-based family therapy, interventions are done to free a person or family from damaging or dysfunctional behaviors and relationships.	When justified by Faith we have peace. -Romans 6.15

3. **Identify the source of change as something other than chance**	The power to change behavior comes from within those individuals who choose to change.	We are saved by Faith and not because of what we do. -Ephesians 2.8
4. **Encourage the individual IP and family members to own the changes**	Personal security lies in letting go of old habits and not losing or discarding stable, supportive relationships. One cannot lose God but can lose or even discard his or her relationship with God.	Faith will make your path in life straight. -Proverbs 3.6
5. **Engage the individual IP and family members in recognizing personal needs, expectations, and goals**	Human needs and expectations can be designed around the willingness to meet those needs and expectations.	For those who have Faith and have an ear then hear what is being said. -Revelation 2.7
6. **Develop and implement a treatment plan that can be superseded by God**	Any plan devised by the practitioner may be well grounded but can always be superseded by God. The therapist only manages the sessions; God controls them.	Trusting God's wisdom and character is faith. -Job

Independent disciplines

It is important to recognize the implications of independent disciplines within theology, just as there are significant independent disciplines within psychology (chapter 2). Throughout the last 300-400 years, conservative scholars have developed two distinct approaches to the history and philosophy of theological thought that work well in faith-based family therapy: Covenant Theology and Progressive Dispensationalism. This text is not a discourse on these theologies. However, it is necessary to address those aspects of each theological position as they might interface with interactional faith-based family therapy.

- *Covenant theology* develops a philosophy of history based on the sovereign rule of God, wherein there are different ways in which God administers His rule over the world based on agreements, or *covenants*. This approach is somewhat limited, since interpretation is based on an attempt to squeeze or integrate interpretive theological specifics into general applications.

- *Progressive dispensationalism* brings the development of relationships to a spiritual and moral level as the interactions between God and humanity move from the general to the specific. Certain eras of exposure are mapped on to how God has and will administer His rule over the world and all those in it.

There are many excellent references and resources for those who want to know more about these two theological positions. Within the context of interactional faith-based family therapy, only the basic premises and their relationship to ethics and family systems are touched on in theology applied to family therapy.

Applied theology

A balanced theological approach to faith-based therapy appears to move from the general view of God' provision of grace to where various specific aspects of His grace are needed and occur. A question of troubling concern people struggle with has always been: if God controls life, how and what do people manage? Answer: because He is God, an all-powerful God can meet any need at any time. God does not need humanity. It is humanity that experiences a deeply embedded need, a yearning for God.

Theological doctrine, defined as a principle, position, or body of principles in a sphere of knowledge or belief systems, can be used to determine attitude and practices related to faith and spiritual need. Therefore, the system of doctrinal orientation to which practitioners are committed does make a difference in how they interact with others and how they practice family therapy. A *doctrine* is a categorization of beliefs, teachings, or instructions of principles or positions, such as the teachings in a specific body of knowledge or beliefs. For example, in Christianity, the central doctrines include belief in God the Father, Jesus Christ as the Son of God, and the Holy Spirit; the death, descent into hell, resurrection, ascension, and coming return of Christ; and, the holiness of the Church, God's chosen people the Jews, and the communion of saints. In systematic theology, some of the related doctrines practitioners and participants may share or impact their understanding and application of theology to practice include:

- First principles (prolegomena)
- Theology proper (existence and attributes of God, *etc.*)
- Theological anthropology (doctrine of humanity)
- Christ Jesus (Christology)
- Justification, sanctification (soteriology)
- Holy Spirit (pneumatology)
- Church (ecclesiology)
- End times, afterlife (eschatology, dispensationalism)

Religion is simply a belief system. Christianity, like all belief systems have variations of theology and expressions of faith within their own doctrines and principles. Even atheism acts as a system of beliefs, for it takes a great deal of faith to believe there is no God. It is important for practitioners to recognize and respect the differences in deeply held beliefs of participants when engaging in faith-based family therapy. Generally, the therapeutic process is not about converting people to a different belief system than the one they have chosen but to help them draw spiritual and emotional strength from the faith that is grounded in those beliefs, of applying their theology to their faith practices within the family system. If the beliefs of the practitioner and the participants are too far removed from one another, it may be necessary to refer the participant family to another family therapist, one with beliefs more aligned with those of the participants.

The purpose of theology in family therapy, then, is to structure and understand the experiences and concepts needed to derive normative individual and family scripts for how people live their lives. In many belief systems, the family unit is recognized and accepted as the basic structure God uses to teach, heal, develop, strengthen, restore, and protect individuals. Therapeutic tools and techniques that affirm, secure, and encourage the family within God's administration are adapted and implemented during therapy, holding the practitioner accountable for facilitating change. This, then, acts as a platform for a theology of family therapy in the interactional faith-based practice model. For example, many practitioners working with families of faith ask God to help them remain humble and avoid the pitfalls of presumptuousness and confinement, so they might better understand God's grace in healing and wholeness for the families they serve.

The best theology in therapy is the one that clarifies and makes a clear statement for understanding the spiritual dimensions of humanity. That theology, then, presents a similarity of function but with an identified Creator God ultimately responsible for absolutes, for grace, forgiveness, salvation, and a final plan void of any chance occurrences. God's plan for salvation and healing is available to everyone as part of His creative relationship with humanity through a faith-based approach to family therapy. God's preferred integrated structures for teaching individuals and families how to behave and live together in harmony with one another and with Him are threefold: marriage, parenting, and family systems.

FAITH AND FICTION

Men will wrangle for religion, write for it, fight for it, die for it, anything but live for it. -Charles Caleb Colton

Many of the problems families of faith encounter begin with an inability to separate faith and fiction when attempting to change dysfunctional behaviors and realign what some might call faulty mental maps. Marriage is the most sacred of human relationships. Except for the relationship between the individual and God, marriage is the only relationship people choose to enter into all by themselves. They do not choose their fathers, mothers, siblings, or biologic relatives. In marriage, a couple generally enters voluntarily into a covenant bond of oneness together. They believe in two people becoming one whole: husband and wife joined together to complete each other physically, mentally, emotionally, and spiritually.

Then the Lord God said, "It is not good for the man to be alone; I will make him a helper suitable for him." … The Lord God fashioned into a woman the rib which He had taken from the man and brought her to the man. The man said, "This is now bone of my bones, and flesh of my flesh; She shall be called Woman, because she was taken out of Man." For this reason, a man shall leave his father and his mother, and be joined to his wife; and they shall become one flesh. -Genesis 2.18, 22-24

A critical skill every faith-based family practitioner needs to be effective is an ability to differentiate between *faith* and *fiction*. In marriages, husbands and wives may enter their new relationships with fictional expectations of one another that interfere with their ability or willingness to communicate accurately and lovingly. This can lead to frustration, anger, and rejection. What happened?

Some years ago, America entered an era of *postmodernism*, which is characterized by pervasive skepticism, subjectivism (or relativism), and a general suspicion of reason and statements of fact, generally embracing ideologies rather than absolutes. Many **people have embraced a** wide-ranging skepticism and relativism. They have a general suspicion of reason and faith. Typically, they express their own beliefs through **atheism, agnosticism, or** by following eastern religion thoughts and practices. *Perception* has been defined as the accepted "reality," creating a desperate need for objectivity and truth to develop and establish healthy realistic perspectives (figure 2.2). The essence of change, then, is moving from dysfunctional dynamics to functional interactions (figure 2.1). Therefore, for all practical reasons, marriages are held together by faith rather than fiction, based in the realities of truth.

In the traditional American models of family counseling and therapy, data and philosophical differences appear to clash between psychology and theology. The interactional faith-based family practitioner focuses on what kind of faith exists between people and within their relationships. Time and again in personal counseling, psychoanalysis, substance abuse counseling, and so many other psychotherapies, one member of a family is selected as the "problem," or identified person/patient (IP). Once that person becomes the issue and focus of the therapeutic plan there can be a change in marital or familial relationship using ownership, communication, and trust interpreted through faith.

For example, some practitioners expect an alcoholic to give up alcohol before first experiencing any possible change. However, unless there is a combination of therapies occurring at the same time, little is accomplished. If addiction work had to be completed before anything else could happen, then soup kitchens and midnight missions would be meaningless—people would have to experience detoxification before changing their behaviors or mental maps, perhaps even before daring to hope change would be possible for them or their loved ones. Faith as a powerful primary change agent imparts addicts with the ability to change even as they are detoxifying and fighting their addiction. The power to change comes from the role of faith introduced by the secondary change agent, which is the practitioner using faith as a modifier.

In another example, an abused woman might not be able to change if all her interpersonal relationships with men, including her relationship with God (a father figure), is corrupted by the abuse she remembers from her human father. He was to have protected and loved her but instead, he destroyed her trust and wounded her deeply. Her subjective perception of males and the betrayal she experienced must be given a different relational perspective before she will allow herself to trust anyone again. She cannot or will not experience faith without a healthy, functional, and forgiving message to get past this event in her life and needs the guidance of an empathetic practitioner and sustaining faith to generate genuine trust.

When practitioners address the fragile intrinsic balance between *relational systems*, they use values and boundaries to encourage faith-driven change in the perceptions and behaviors in family systems. The practitioners' skills for changing fiction to faith are embedded in their ability to model trust, forgiveness, and acceptance by using faith as a construct for change.

IN CONCLUSION

Faith, the complete trust or confidence in someone or something that may or may not be based on concrete evidence or proof, is not a prescriptive approach or technique for doing therapy. There is a real danger in doing interactional faith-based family therapy when practitioners believe faith is only a series of proclamations about what participants believe related to God, spirituality, or religious doctrines, for example. When practitioners try to classify all treatment plans and participant needs as the same and focus on convincing individuals to have faith in a particular belief system, the technique only lodges the information in the more passive "must do" areas of the brain rather than in the active "I was called to make a decision" area of the brain. Therapy can then become more about the practitioner than about the participants.

Therapeutic interventions should never be prescriptive. Similar issues are never the same issues. For example, *social constructionism*, the idea that individuals develop within a social context beyond the family, is not only subject to outside sociopolitical motives and fictional narratives but often substitute such narratives for the spiritual dimension altogether. More important than political and prescriptive treatment plans is the practitioner's ability to present customized healthy perspectives to participants and family units about the profound power of primary change through faith and ethical practice.

ETHICS

A person who is fundamentally honest doesn't need a code of ethics. The Ten Commandments and the Sermon on the Mount are all the ethical code anybody needs. -Harry S. Truman

Ethical faith-based family therapy requires adherence to ethical principles practitioners frequently encounter, whether working with an individual or a family. All therapists practice within a code of ethics and abide by legal standards associated with their work. Issues such as confidentiality and standards of practice affecting all areas of therapy have been designed to protect the public from faulty or ineffectual forms of therapy, *e.g.,* Regressive Therapy, *etc.* Regulatory Boards today emphasize the need for ethics and special training for licensing therapists.

A *code of ethics* is a set of principles of conduct that guide decision making and behavior (figure 5.2). Applying ethical and legal rules in practice is essential to the safe and caring implementation of interactional faith-based family therapy. Most codes specify conduct that is honest, fair, competent, and benign (Bullock & Sangeeta, 2003). Practitioners provide professional guidance, safe instructions and tasks including analysis without bias.

Figure 5.2: Ethical principles		
Focus	**Definition**	**Examples**
Autonomy	Personal freedom, right of self-determination	Provide only the guidance participants require to be successful and allow for exploration of behaviors and actions influencing the family dynamics
Beneficence	Duty to have best interests of recipient or participant as the goal of any actions or decisions	Assist participants to understand the ethical standards that apply to their situation; ensure safe and beneficial tasks for therapeutic interventions and activities
Non-maleficence	Duty to prevent intention harm; sometimes combined with beneficence and presented as a single ethical principle; based on Hippocratic maxim *First do no harm*	Test decisions and actions by asking, "Could my decision or actions cause harm in any way?"
Veracity	Truth-telling	Engage in honest, bidirectional conversation, encouragement, and exploration of identified problems and situations; support concerns and invite questions; explore false conduct or misrepresentations, behaviors, and comments immediately to correct any deviations from truth
Justice	Fairness; treating all persons equally	All decisions, activities, and behaviors are just, guided by truth, reason, equity, and fairness
Paternalism	Telling others what to think or what is best, often without considering their input; treating people in a fatherly (paternal) manner; a form of control vs influence over behaviors and actions	Practitioners who want to help, advise, or protect may neglect individual choice and personal responsibility, causing a participant or family to become disengaged in the process

Fidelity	Duty to keep one's promises and commitments	Provide factual accuracy in sharing or reporting information; keep promises, *e.g.*, keeping appointments and following up with agreed-upon tasks
Respect for others	Duty to treat all with thoughtfulness, consideration, and without bias, or prejudice	Determine which rules, obligations, and values should direct the choices of practitioners and participants; recognize the abilities and limitations of others, *e.g.*, when respecting a participant's judgment in a given situation

Source: Adapted from Swihart, D., & Figueroa, S. (2014). The preceptor program builder: Essential tools for a successful preceptor program. Danvers, MA: HCPro; p35.

Some family therapists have made notable advances toward professional autonomy in recent years. This greater autonomy has created more of a demand for responsibility and accountability for the consequences of professional decisions and actions. Therapists can continue to improve themselves by:

1. Developing and adopting codes of ethics, which provide guidelines for defining responsibility and found in membership in professional organizations such as AAMFT;

2. Setting rigorous qualifications and criteria for certification and/ or licensure for entry into and sustaining a practice in continuing education;

3. Establishing peer review procedures or maintaining contact with others in practice; and,

4. Setting standards of practice such as those related to therapeutic approaches, philosophical and theological assumptions, with ethical responsibilities.

There are many resources available for further study in this important area. Many are grounded in humanist ethical analysis and tend towards helping practitioners develop ways of thinking about complex ethical issues and dilemmas in counseling and therapy without addressing determinants of right and wrong. A major difficulty with such resources for faith-based family therapy is their authors' underlying belief that there could be no definite, clear-cut solutions to ethical dilemmas. This indecisiveness is generally base this assumption on the teachings of philosophers such as Socrates, Plato, and Aristotle, who struggled with two main ethical questions:

1. What is the meaning of right or good?
2. What should I do?

Faith-based family therapists adhere to a theology in therapy that allows for such questions but with an important difference: they work with a set of determinants of right and wrong found in faith-based values. Malpractice issues, such as *negligence* (failing to do enough for the client) and other ethical concerns, are predicated on the ability of practitioners and participants to differentiate between right and wrong. Practitioners are responsible ethically for recognizing situations requiring ethical, professional, and practice decisions, and guiding participants through ethical dilemmas that arise within the family system related to dysfunctional or disruptive behaviors.

Ethics in faith-based family practice call for a practitioner's balanced personality and all of one's knowledge and abilities to bear on a genuine concern for participants' well-being in general. Ethics are folded into the meaning of human experience specifically. Professional ethics determine standards of practice and reflect personal and professional integrity. Ethics is more than a personal or inspirational arena for addressing moral questions. Moral judgments are most highly developed when the process of arriving at them and the reasons for believing in them are clear and convincing. They are grounded in the practitioner's theology in both therapy and ethics.

For people of the Christian faith, ethics demand individual responsibility and accountability to God, as well. The interactional faith-based family therapist uses the interactional approach to clarify goals and values according to the picture provided by the person of faith or family members and their relationships with God. For example, many recognize Jesus genuinely cared for people who sought out and readily complied with his guidance. Because of the warmth and personal concern for others, people responded without fear—whether he was confronting or encouraging them,

Practitioners must remember, too, that a breach of ethics can result in legal accountabilities and action. For an example, if a practitioner has an office in a building with several offices and the cleaning crew has one key that unlocks all the offices to clean the offices, the therapist needs to put a separate lock on his or her door. This is to protect a participant's private information and avoid an ethical violation related to a breach of confidentiality costing the therapist approximately $5.

IN CONCLUSION

Theology, faith and fiction, and ethics all draw on philosophical implications, limitations, and anomalies when folded into interactional faith-based family therapy. Books could be written on the meaning and implications of ethics and theology in relationship to doing therapy. Many practitioners of faith-based therapies struggle with the integration of psychology and theology found in legal and ethical regulations and mandates around their practice while working with families of faith.

The Bible says people are created in the image of God. The Evolutionist is still attempting to prove man came from the sea and could possibly grow back arms and legs like their ancestors did millions of years ago. They are more - physically, mentally, and spiritually with an innate need for relationships. The interactional faith-based family practitioner must understand and embrace his or her own beliefs and adhere to ethical practices before there can be any congruence when working with families of faith. This becomes more evident in the next chapter as theory, technique, and practice are brought together in building and implementing the fundamental treatment plan.

CHAPTER 6:
Treatment Plans & Doing Therapy

PRAGMATIC AND *PARADOXICAL PRAGMATIC* APPROACHES TO INTERACTIONAL FAITH-BASED FAMILY THERAPY

Theory, technique, and practice are oftentimes confusing in isolation and require a plan before they can be used in treatment or therapy. It is usually referred to as a *treatment plan*. To begin constructing a plan for therapy, it is important to recognize that how people do things differs from why they do them. There are two elements in the *pragmatics*, the management of interactions between practitioners and participants, in interactional faith-based family therapy to observe the *how* and to discover the *why* of dysfunction of mental maps and behaviors and broken relationships within family systems:

- Pragmatic approach
- Paradoxical pragmatic approach

The treatment plan uses multiple techniques to help guide the process and reorient the practitioner and participants during the process of doing therapy. Theory determines techniques, which works similarly to driving a car from Point A to point B, already knowing and feeling confident in one's approach (theory), ability to drive (techniques), and destination (goals). A plan acts as a basis from which to estimate progress and make decisions for getting to the intended outcomes. In therapy, the practitioner determines the distance traveled and the route taken towards healing. This plan can be altered or even abandoned anywhere along the way for another, more promising one, as the therapeutic process unfolds.

Although there are many ways to develop plans using various theories and techniques, this chapter discusses a single basic plan for practitioners to follow. The treatment plan presented in this book does not fit all situations nor is it intended to. It focuses more on cognitive feedback from participants within the family system. This process must be implemented carefully by the practitioner to prevent the plan or selected techniques from interfering with altered mental maps and behaviors seen in participants or family systems during or following therapy.

Generally, all treatment plans are signed and dated initially by both the practitioner and the participants and dated again for when it needs to be reviewed. Licensing and regulating Boards have certain requirements that need to be adhered to by those licensed in counseling and family therapy. All plans must adhere to legal and ethical guidelines for practitioners, respect the beliefs and cultural norms of the participants, and focus on the relationships within the family system when selecting techniques to initiate or facilitate change. The treatment plan for interactional faith-based family practice builds on the NEG reality model of therapy based on Needs, Expectations, and Goals. Frequent reviews for correction, confirmation, and continuance help practitioners determine the direction of the therapy and identify strategic changes needed to keep moving the process forward positively. (Figure 6.1)

Figure 6.1. NEG methodology of interactional intervention	
Process element	**Purpose**
Needs	1. Increases self-worth and self-esteem 2. Develops boundaries 3. Clarifies purpose 4. Validates values
Expectations	1. Opens negotiations 2. Improves communications 3. Objectifies behavior 4. Qualifies understanding
Goals	1. Tests realistic expectations 2. Evaluates personal progress 3. Measures actual concurrences 4. Solidifies necessary commitments
Review for	• Correction • Confirmation • Continuance

Reality and clarification of faith-based family therapy (NEG): Needs–Expectations–Goals

Although NEG is a reality model of therapy, it is not predicated on *Reality Therapy*, which was founded by the psychiatrist, William Glasser. Glasser's approach was basically an introduction to a psychodynamic, anti-Freudian methodology called *Choice Therapy*. His model was reality-based but did not address family systems specifically, rejecting outside influences such as family systems, and asserting that individuals are all and always in control of their own choices with behavior driven by internal controls (Doring, 2017). The authors' NEG methodology recognizes the external role of family systems in individual and family communication, behaviors, and relationships.

In interactional faith-based family therapy theory, clarification in communication is anchored to reality and the individual. Relationships and goals become realistic as faith facilitates genuine and lasting change within the family system. The strategy for real life clarification folded into the faith-based approach to family therapy combines faith, trust, and the verification of realistic and positive change with participants' ability to change their mental maps and freely choose healthy behaviors and meaningful relationships.

Practitioners implementing interventions must tread gently to avoid abandoning responsible behavior when seeking or giving clarity to participants when identifying their needs, expectations, and goals within the context of a therapeutic relationship. Treatment plans depend on bringing clarity to individuals and interactional, interpersonal exchanges among family members. Clearly identifying communication processes in family systems is a crucial part of therapy. To do so, it is important to recognize the differences and how to strategically address them within the family system implementing pragmatic and paradoxical pragmatic approaches.

PRAGMATIC APPROACHES

It's not the load that weighs you down, it's the way you carry it. –C.S. Lewis

The *pragmatic approach*, the management of linguistic interactions between practitioners and participants, refers to the therapeutic process of navigating and facilitating positive behavioral effects through human communication in faith-based family therapy. It includes the study of language and meaning derived from context and dependent on the goals of the speaker, expectations of the receiver, and context of interactive communication. Let's look more closely at the NEG methodology for this approach.

PRAGMATIC NEG MODEL: NEEDS

Many individuals and families confuse *Needs* with *Wants*. One can argue with wants but not needs. Clarity of NEEDS acts as a basis for change. Since a personal need also identifies an individual's personal values and boundaries, the place to start therapy is around the question, "What do you need as a person to be who you are?" A NEG participant clarification statement might be: "I need to have a healthy relationship and expect this relationship to meet all my needs, so I will have a better direction or goal."

1. The practitioner asks the participants to take home a Needs Clarification Worksheet (see appendix A). Several examples of needs derived from filling in the worksheet are provided in figure 6.2. When discussing the needs identified by participants, practitioners explain that there is a difference between a need and a want. For example: "I might want a corvette, but I need transportation. I might want a lot of money, but I need to pay my bills". Participants may choose examples from the list provided by the practitioner or write their own. They are then directed to list a new need every day for a week on the worksheet. Participants may send their lists to the practitioner for suggestions and to make sure they are real needs and not wants. The therapy becomes a reality when each person states, "I need… so I can…"

2. When participants return with their lists after having clarified their needs with the practitioner or another person if not a family member, it is reviewed in session. The practitioner ensures the needs are positive needs of each individual or family member. One cannot expand or build on negative needs or needs attached to others if those needs are to be clearly understood. The focus is on the needs of the participant, because only his or her needs are accessible for clarity, understanding, and change in therapy. For example, an appropriate positive need would be seen in the difference between "wanting sex, so I can feel good and have pleasure, and needing intimacy so I can be fulfilled as a man/woman".

3. Indirectly, needs also translate into personal boundaries and values. For example, when a need for "integrity" is expressed, the boundary of integrity is identified as important when making decisions in life and building or maintaining healthy relationships.

Figure 6.2. SAMPLE positive needs an individual might have			
I need		**so I can**	
I need	an open and honest relationship	**so I can**	express myself and be myself honestly
I need	a best friend to confide in	**so I can**	learn more of who I am
I need	to trust someone	**so I can**	be vulnerable and learn how to love
I need	to be forgiven when i make mistakes	**so I can**	be encouraged to keep trying and growing
I need	acceptance of my whole person	**so I can**	be complete
I need	to be a best friend	**so I can**	know the depths of my ability to give and love
I need	to make a commitment to someone or something	**so I can**	experience being successful at following through with my life
I need	to find my purpose in life	**so I can**	be the best person God created me to be (*spiritual gifts*)
I need	to be true to my values	**so I can**	have positive self regard
I need	to have dreams	**so I can**	reach beyond my self-set limits
I need	to know what I want	**so I can**	share that clearly
I need	to be truthful without fear of others' response	**so I can**	be calm and not build up anger
I need	to share mutual friendships and responsibilities with my mate	**so I can**	have a sense of self that is consistent and be part of a complete picture
I need	to share my life dreams with someone who has similar dreams	**so I can**	be reinforced to build those hopes into a reality
I need	intimacy in a relationship	**so I can**	give and receive love
I need	to be honest with myself	**so I can**	learn to be honest with others.

I need	time for myself	so I can	evaluate my own personal needs
I need	to know I am making a significant contribution to my family or life in general	so I can	experience a sense of belonging and connectedness
I need	to be responsible to connect with others as a friend or a family member	so I can	contribute to someday soon building my feelings of oneness
I need	a special relationship with those I consider to be like family	so I can	experience a feeling of fullness in my life
I need	assurance that I am sensitive to the needs of others that I care about	so I can	relax and feel I am doing my best
I need	to find in some way a special respect for my parent(s)	so I can	understand what it means to honor them
I need	to trust others like certain members of my family or close friends	so I can	learn to trust myself
I need	to have goals and plans for my own life	so I can	balance my involvement in other relationships without compromising my personal boundaries
I need	to know more about what I believe about God and how I express my faith	so I can	understand how God fits into my life and relationships with Him, with my mate, and with my family members
I need	to be on time for appointments	so I can	feel good about how I spend my time
I need		so I can	

PRAGMATIC NEG MODEL: EXPECTATIONS

Once the needs are clarified, the next step is to negotiate expectations (appendix B). Expectations are different than needs in that they are action oriented. The clarified needs are added to a sentence to develop an expectation. The sentence is:

I expect (name)_____ *to* (do something)_____
and in turn, I will (do something) _____
(need of other person).

The pivotal part of the negotiated expectation is changed from "so that I can" to "and in turn, I will" One example would be:

"I expect my mate to be faithful to me and in turn, I will be the kind of support my husband/wife needs and God expects me to be."

The key is that expectations are negotiated. Anything else would be controlling and may be interpreted as ultimatums, demands, or mandates. If such controlling demands are made of others, participants and family members may respond by becoming angry and bitter, even to the point of disengaging from the process. At this point, practitioners guide the therapeutic interaction away from such negative behaviors and towards negotiated expectations related to previously identified positive needs. Expectations comprise and define the major themes people use in managing their lives as they learn to meet their needs. Examples of reasonable expectations participants might have in their marriages help clarify what this might look like in marital relationships (figure 6.3a; appendix C) and other relationships (figure 6.3b; appendix D). Worksheets are provided in the appendices.

Figure 6.3a. Examples of reasonable expectations in MARRIAGE	
I expect my mate to be:	Someone who will love me
	Someone whom I can love, who will respond to my love
	Someone to relieve loneliness, to participate with me in things, to share in at least some of my interests and activities
	Someone to talk with, who will be understanding of my feelings, and moods, who will show respect for my opinions, although not necessarily always agree with me; someone I can confide in (*communication*)
	Someone I can admire and look up to, whose values I can respect
	Someone who will respect my values and ambitions
	Someone who will accept me and appreciate me just as I am, who will admire me, and make me feel needed and important while I make responsible changes in my life
	Someone who will encourage me, be emotionally supportive to me and give me self-confidence
	Someone who will help support me financially
	Someone who will help me make decisions
	Someone who will share my faith
	Someone who is sexually responsive to me, to whom I can give sexual satisfaction
	Someone to give me sexual satisfaction
	Someone to help me in the rearing of the children (*sharing in the work and responsibilities of parenthood*)
	Someone who is faithful to me, so I can be the person God wants me to be
I expect my spouse to:	_____ _____ **and in turn I will** _____ _____ **(add spouse's need)** _____ _____ _____

Figure 6.3b. Examples of reasonable expectations in a RELATIONSHIP	
I expect those I care about to be:	Someone who will show me respect
	Someone who will respond to me
	Someone to relieve loneliness, to participate with me in things, to share in at least some of my interests and activities
	Someone who will share my faith
	Someone to talk with, who will understand my feelings and moods, who will show respect for my opinions, although not necessarily always agree with me
	Someone I can admire and look up to, whose values I can respect
	Someone who will respect my values and ambitions
	Someone who will accept me and appreciate me just as I am, who will admire, me, and make me feel needed and important while I make responsible changes in my life
	Someone who will help support my emotional needs
	Someone who will help support my spiritual needs
	Someone who will help me make decisions when I ask them
	Someone who supports my need to accept my responsibilities
	Someone to help me share common responsibilities
	Someone who will be honest with me when I am wrong
I expect (this person)	(name) _____ to _____ _____ and in turn I will _____ _____ _____ (help him/her meet his/her relational need) _____ _____ _____

PRAGMATIC NEG MODEL: GOALS

If you aim at nothing you will hit it every time. -Zig Ziglar

After the completed negotiation of expectations, it is time to set goals. This is the litmus test of the effectiveness of the treatment plan. Setting goals that reflect the individual, the couple, and the family, now legitimizes the plan. At this point, any goal-setting workbook can be used with the clarified needs and negotiated expectations. The needs and expectations are only the boundaries—and possibly reflections—of the content of therapy if the goals are practical (appendix E).

Goals are measurable, inclusive, and give direction. However, they are not a mark of success or failure because they can be extended or changed as therapy progresses. Their purpose is to enable practitioners to evaluate the progress of the therapy and determine closure for the participants and family members. *Oneness* recognizes uniqueness and individuality in each participant or family member that is relational and manageable. *Sameness* locks them into conformity, competitiveness, and control. For example, when a family seeks oneness, the goal calls for measuring oneness more so than behavioral sameness within familial relationships.

Once the participants have completed their progression within the treatment plan, the practitioner and the family validate that the family members now have an established interactional structure for functional behavior that promotes oneness within the familial relationships. The energy needed to accomplish this is passion.

Passion

Passions are the motivators in life and are more defined than goals. They are a source of energy used to employ change and an important part of therapy. Passions provide the necessary dynamism to accomplish the process of identifying needs and expectations accurately so personal goals can become realistic and achievable outcomes.

Pragmatic conclusion

When one door closes, another opens; but we often look so long and so regretfully upon the closed door that we do not see the one that has opened for us. -Alexander Graham Bell

The *outcome* establishes the effectiveness of the goals. Either the relationships are terminated; or, the members of a family reassess and change their negotiated expectations and begin the process with newly clarified needs and expectations. The decision rests with the participants to end the change process or to continue. From the moment therapy begins, interventions and activities move the participants toward oneness. If oneness has not been satisfactorily achieved by the conclusion of therapy—or the experience of oneness at some level has not taken place—the participants must consider what other options are available to them to allow them to either experience oneness in their relationships or to settle for struggling with sameness.

PRAGMATIC PARADOXICAL APPROACH

The *pragmatic paradoxical* approach (Hwang, 2001) addresses participant behaviors resulting from responses to a double bind or contradictory situation and comprises three elements resulting in untenable positions for the participant or other members within the family system:

1. A strong complementary relationship (*e.g.*, parent-child; superior-subordinate; practitioner-participant)

2. Within this relationship, a mandate is given which must be obeyed but must be disobeyed to be obeyed (*e.g.*, a practitioner tells a

participant to keep doing something he or she is already doing, but now the participant must choose to do it, whereas previously he or she may have been attempting to evade confusion or responsibility)

3. The participant is unable to step outside the frame of the mandate or directive and dissolve the paradox by responding differently

The pragmatic paradoxical approach in family therapy calls for the practitioner to find practical ways to see behaviors, actions, or events differently by considering the opposite after the more practical or pragmatic view has been assessed. The paradox is a valuable tool. Using it accurately is an art and requires the practitioner to be cautious in how it is introduced into sessions.

Thus far, doing therapy consists of clarifying personal needs, negotiating expectations, and setting personal and family goals. Inserting the pragmatic paradox into the process extends the session and introduces more techniques for working with faith-based families.

The pragmatic paradox as a reframe

The paradoxical pragmatic approach in doing therapy *reframes*, or expresses differently, what is occurring within the family system. It is generally based on collaboration and leveraging a tension of opposites in processing the participant's changed perspective or behavior (Watzlawick, Bavelas, & Jackson, 2011).

Within the paradox concept, there are two general techniques used in psychotherapy and family practice: syncing up and detaching.

- *Syncing up*: Conscience and sub-conscience form the paradox, as in hypnotherapy tending toward psychodynamic models with an emphasis on the individual mind set regarding emotions
- *Detaching*: Flooding individual emotions (*factors*) and moving beyond them after recognizing negative or positive effects, then purposely detaching from them while attaching to a more secure

support model; the paradox can be explored if the support element is stable, *e.g.*, "I can think of something in a negative light because I know my personal integrity is over-ruling any distraction"

Paradoxical pragmatic NEG model: NEEDS

Philosophically, when personal space is identified as a personal need, participants are directly asked to modify their personal identity. For example, when personal space is violated, the participant might consider camping out in the backyard or using the neighbor's spare bedroom for a night when wanting or needing to be left alone while living with others in the same house. Another example of paradoxical needs, when there is a need to de-stress:

- I need to make sure my body is stressed in order to make money;

- I need money so when I get older I can spend money on restoring my health; so,

- I need to live as if I will never die and die as if I never lived.

Paradoxical pragmatic NEG model: EXPECTATIONS

When something is not occurring in the space allotted for communication between thinking and response, suggesting the opposite of what is expected can help participants find a clear basic statement between thinking and emotions. For example, when there are certain expectations a participant wants others to understand about him or her:

- I expect others to want to read my new Children's Book I just wrote because it is well thought out;

- I expect people to treat me like I am nobody important; so,

- If I am anything, I am a mistake.

Paradoxical pragmatic NEG model: GOAL

In personal space there is one significant phrase that justifies a purpose. Goals are directions and targets rather than successes. Therefore, they are not a mark of success or failure. For example, when there are certain goals one knows one should make, they might look like this:

- "Gain at least 5 pounds before the next session in two weeks."
- "Write down 5 legitimate reasons for skipping church on Sunday."
- "Argue only with those who refuse to speak with you."

Paradoxical pragmatic conclusion

A *paradox* is a behavior, communication, or action that is self-contradictory, seemingly impossible or difficult to understand because of the inclusion of two opposite facts or characteristics, *i.e.*, when two different opinions collide in one statement or action. Every type of therapy requires a backup treatment plan and contacts for potential referrals, if needed. The purpose of interactive faith-based family therapy is to provide participants a safe and healthy process for change.

Once the work has been done regarding needs, expectations, and goals, the collected information remains viable but may entail arrangements in different perspectives. Not everyone is equipped to view a paradox as a communication exercise and may prefer to avoid using that technique. Any approach that is interpreted as negative or disrespectful can be dangerous if not carefully and skillfully applied to the situation or activities. In such cases, or if the practitioner does not feel comfortable implementing this technique, he or she should choose another, more pragmatic approach by reflecting on participants' already clarified needs, negotiated expectations, and established goals.

EVALUATION AND SUMMARY

In the final stage of the treatment plan, the participants evaluate if they have achieved oneness or a form of sameness to build into their relationships. Oneness affords each participant or family member uniqueness and individuality that is relational and manageable. Regardless of what the participants choose to do, they will have clarity regarding each family member's needs, expectations, and directions expressed as goals. Sameness (conformity, competitiveness, and control) may encompass the very behaviors that disrupted the family system in the first place. The therapeutic objective, then, is to identify and facilitate oneness in the familial relationships. The practitioner does not have to evaluate or point out a decision. The participants make their own decisions. The concepts of oneness and sameness, then, need to be an integral part of the treatment plan and negotiated by the practitioner and the participants.

The ability to achieve oneness rather than sameness is critical to the theology of therapy and familial relationships. For example, the sexual union between a husband and wife clearly illustrates this process of oneness. Every human being possesses the capacity to experience union in the sex act and the pleasure of orgasm resulting from that union as biologically designed. The sexual union between most men and women of faith has historically been viewed as a spiritual experience, as well as one of physical pleasure. This deeply emotional, physical, and spiritual event (*i.e.*, the joining of two humans into one experience of singularity) points us to the possibility of oneness. For people of faith, it is a reflection of what such oneness with God might be like.

Today, many people engage in egocentric, controlling approaches to sameness in relationships that corrupt or destroy oneness. The need to control overshadows and limits the manageability of interpersonal adjustments to actions or events. Anxiety, fear, depression, selfishness, and game-playing have become so prevalent in our world that panic has become a common illness and dysfunctional behaviors the norm for many relationships. The participants' goal in any healthy familial relationship is to learn how to manage behaviors and actions rather than to control one another. It is imperative therefore, that practitioners understand these concepts and guide rather than control their participants' behaviors or thoughts when doing therapy.

DOING THERAPY

Doing therapy is about pulling the technique of focused questions and treatment plans into the NEG pragmatic and paradoxical pragmatic approaches to faith-based family practice, combining an ahistorical process and a theology of therapy to bring about healing of dysfunctional behaviors and perspectives with healing and restoration of familial relationships. Practitioners begin by establishing objectives for the therapy.

OBJECTIVES

Objectives are the targets, goals, or outcomes connected to why and how people seek and engage in therapy. When working with families of faith— or families with members of faith—practitioners explore their beliefs, God's love and grace, the effectiveness of changed behavior, and practical applications of therapeutic processes in meeting participants' needs, expectations, and goals. This involves setting objectives, assessing presenting problems and belief structures, implementing a plan, assigning tasks, and reviewing participant responses.

Doing therapy, then, is an introduction to ideas. It is not about presenting a unique model with individual psychotherapeutic or religious techniques. Greater specificity of these for doing other types of therapy can be learned by reviewing multiple resources with many different family therapy orientations (see Bibliography). What makes their orientations "faith-based" are grounded in the work of practitioners who read the materials, study them, and apply them in a context of faith. As surgeons do not have "faith-based" instruments to make them faith-based surgeons, neither do the faith-based family practitioners have a "faith-based" tool or technique for doing therapy.

However, the faith of the therapist is the most important part of the faith-based family therapy approach. Even the Apostle Paul used resources available to him at that time other than those from the Scripture record when comforting others.

When you come bring the cloak which I left at Troas with Carpus, and the books, especially the parchments. (2 Timothy 4.13)

Interactional faith-based family therapists attempt to facilitate change from a relational position between and among people. In perspective, practitioners speak indirectly to participants for the sake of change in faulty mental maps and problematic behaviors. Faith-based therapy is not an evangelistic program or indoctrination into a dogma, doctrine, or faith system. Therapy does not save people or prepare them to meet God. It is a process to help people reach their full potential, providing an opportunity for participants to encounter and embrace a personal relationship with one another through the lens of their faith.

The *art*, the more qualitative and subjective aspect of therapy, now becomes evident and acceptable as practitioners continually revises strategies to better conceptualize relevant patterns and avoid failure while reflecting their own non-descriptive faith. Practitioners can fail when they are unable or unwilling to recognize that opposition (*i.e.*, resistance, sabotage, or avoidance) will occur. Failure can also take place when no opposition occurs. Importantly, though, without opposition, needed change may not occur at all.

Practitioners with an interactional perspective must take responsibility for inducing changes in mental maps and problematic behavior patterns affecting relationships within the family structure. Before beginning therapy with most participants, therapists should consider the following questions to conceptualize positive and effective strategies:

1. Who will oppose this therapy?

2. If they do, what part of the therapy will they oppose?

3. How should I redesign any opposition and fold it into the therapeutic process?

To "jump start" therapy that is not progressing toward intended change, practitioners must ask themselves the following:

1. What am I not seeing? -OR- What am I missing?

2. What part of my faith is not showing? -OR- What part of my faith is showing?

3. How might I be phrasing the question incorrectly or inaccurately?

4. Given partial results have occurred, what needs to happen next?

These questions illustrate how interactive faith-based family therapists might think about presenting problems and interruptions in the forward progress of the therapy. Then, based on a few simple assumptions, they can verbally and nonverbally perform their purposes in-session to facilitate an opportunity to reframe the presenting problem, which may be needed to advance the therapy. At this point, practitioners may realize the presenting problem is not the real problem.

PRESENTING PROBLEMS—DIRECT VS. INDIRECT ASSESSMENT

Without a presenting problem, how does the practitioner:

1. Plan a reframe?

2. Understand resistance?

3. Develop a paradox?

Reframing *presenting problems*, the initial symptoms or behaviors for which a participant or family seeks therapy, involves encouraging every participant who wants to change to move in that direction. It may not be the way other family members want an identified participant to change but may be guided in considering new perspectives and options.

Practitioners enter the process knowing the presenting problem might not be the actual problem. The first question asked of the participants should be: "Why now?" Or "What has occurred recently and how long ago?" Carefully consider the words participants use to respond and those events they focus on, *e.g.*, fights, job changes, return to school or work, births or deaths, marriages, divorce, or separations. These questions can be asked directly or indirectly. *Indirectly*, practitioners might request less specific information, *e.g.*, "Give me a picture of the family and the changes that have taken place recently."

Practitioners also need to know the consequences relative to the presenting problem. Therefore, the second question would be indirectly: "What gets accomplished, and what does not get accomplished when this [presenting problem] occurs?" Or asked *directly*: "What does the presenting problem do to cause the family or other relationships or activities to fail?"

Finally, practitioners ask the participants, "What happens when the problem occurs or continues without resolution?" When the participants respond, does one person get more attention than the others? Who reacts? How do they react? This is often the situation practitioners need to create to develop a sequence of interactions within the context of the presenting problem to expose the real problem or extent of it. For example:

1. Rebellion in children is sometimes indicative of a desire or need for a different relationship with a parent

2. Most women want their husbands to understand them spiritually, not just to know them physically or emotionally though they may not know how to express this desire

You husbands in the same way, live with your wives in an understanding way,… and show her honor as a fellow heir of the grace of life… -1 Peter 3:7

There is no emphasis on correctly labeling behavior or mental maps attached to the presenting problem according to some model, process orientation, religion, or absolute interpretation of a healthy life. The emphasis rests only on altering the behavior patterns and their concomitant mental maps and spiritual perspectives. This allows practitioners to work through the faith and belief structures of the individual within the context of positive functional familial relationships.

BELIEF STRUCTURE

The outcome of therapy rests on effectively changing the faulty mental maps and dysfunctional patterns of behavior that produced the presenting problem. Practitioners do not have a primary objective of disciplining or proselytizing (*i.e.*, attempting to convert participants from their own faith practices or beliefs to that of the therapist). There are others appointed for those purposes within the families' faith systems and networks. However, the character and beliefs of practitioners will be evidenced in practice, *e.g.*, in their personal applications of their faith when it comes to change, God's grace, forgiveness, hope, and restoration of relationships.

Once practitioners assess the presenting problem, belief structure, and family system, they then have specific information for developing a treatment plan for facilitating change of dysfunctional interactions within the participants' familial environment. In family therapy, practitioners implement a *cognitive perspective*, which reflects their belief structures and is evidenced in their attitude, demeanor, integrity, sense of wellbeing, personal faith, and trust in therapeutic processes and strategic mental mapping. They move the therapeutic process forward from cognitive and behavior issues by engaging their faith and the faith of the participants to conjointly support healthy relationships and family systems.

For individuals of faith, the family-level perspective acts as a filter, determining the meaning of events and situations, which dictates reactive responses to certain behaviors. For example, depending on the family's history, spiritual background, and socioeconomic culture, events are interpreted according to functional or dysfunctional beliefs (mental maps). They may be functional in their ability to keep the family intact; and yet, to those outside the family, behavior reflecting those beliefs would be considered dysfunctional or unhealthy. An example of this would be spanking children in a society that views spanking as another form of child abuse. Similarly, treating an individual within the interactional perspective may erroneously assume that person has an environmental reaction to a perception.

In effect, interactional faith-based family therapy, seeks to alter the participants' beliefs (faulty mental maps) grounded in their faith and reflected in problematic behaviors. These *mental maps* in family therapy represent one's perception, opinion, personal preferences, or viewpoint of faith, familial interactions and behaviors, beliefs and relationships. Practitioners may seek to change dysfunctional or chaotic beliefs directly or by changing the presenting problem. In other words, they can change the behavior and anticipate it will allow a faulty belief structure to be less valid and subsequently unnecessary, or they can attempt to change both the behavior and the belief structure simultaneously. For example, spanking is often seen as *punishment* to inflict retribution for offending rather than *discipline* to teach obedience and moral character in self-control. Therefore, finding a substitute form of discipline, which is inherent in the belief structure of a participant, might create a different yet more meaningful message to family members.

Ultimately, the presenting problem must change, and its underlying belief structure altered enough to allow the dysfunctional or disruptive behavior to become unnecessary. For example, participants may suffer from extreme guilt arising from frequent interactions with aggressive family members who frequently or continuously accuse or condemn them for their beliefs or behaviors. When those family members' belief systems are shifted so they recognize and become convicted (*i.e.*, changing their firmly held beliefs or opinions) for their actions, their behaviors towards the participants are affected and become more constructive and caring.

This is seen in the basic tenets of the Christian faith, for example, which teaches that people of faith are to be convicted. This conviction always carries an interpretation of providing a "way out" of a situation instead of dwelling on guilt or allocating blame.

No temptation has overtaken you but such as is common to man; and God is faithful, who will not allow you to be tempted beyond what you are able, but with the temptation will provide the way of escape also, so that you will be able to endure it. (1 Corinthians 10.13)

Thus, conviction always provides a potential escape. Guilt and fear evolve from questionable origins and paralyze individuals, whether real or imagined. The Christian believer—and anyone of faith who accepts this truth—is free to make positive behavior changes based on healthier mental maps predicated on genuine conviction related to healthy thinking and behaviors.

There is no guarantee, though, that conviction will occur for all participants. Some aggressive or hurtful family members who hold to their belief structures may continue to perpetuate verbal attacks, for example, on participants during or after therapy. Practitioners then prepare those participants for re-entry into a family system with members who might choose to remain psychologically and theologically dysfunctional in their lack of ownership for their own behaviors and unwillingness to positively change. This is true of participants from all faiths and religions, including many Christians.

THE PROCESS

The total process of doing therapy (see figure 6.4), including managing interventions, techniques, and maneuvers, requires a distinct methodology wherein practitioners have the isomorphic freedom to shift strategies as needed. This process begins at the first contact with participants and travels bi-directionally along a continuum of three distinct procedures: assessment, instilling doubt about the way things are, and introducing patterns of change.

Figure 6.4. Total process for doing therapy:

Assessment <<>> Instilling doubt about how things are <<>> Introducing patterns of change

←———————————————————————————————————————→

Assessment occurs throughout treatment as the construct of the presenting problem continually reshapes itself. It is constantly being updated with new information about the way tasks are responded to within and outside of the therapy sessions. The assessment part of the process of doing therapy considers two types of interactional questions: (a) questions that deal with behavioral interaction patterns, and (b) those that deal with family belief structures. This is done in preparation for facilitating behavioral and cognitive belief changes. Questions for each element of the assessment include:

1. <u>Behavioral interaction pattern questions</u>:

    a. Who does what? When?

    b. Who responds to whom? When? How?

2. <u>Family belief structure questions</u>:

    a. How does the family think as a unit?

    b. How does the family hierarchy relate to their stated beliefs?

    c. What alignments and coalitions exist within the family unit? (Minuchin & Fishman, 1981)

    d. How does the language of the family reflect their beliefs?

    e. What are their beliefs about the cause of the problem?
    — Trouble maker
    — Chemical imbalance
    — Satan or demons
    — Friends
    —Parenting skills

    f. What are their beliefs about the expected cure?
    — God
    — Prayer
    — Medication
    — Hospitalization (*e.g.*, psychiatric care)
    — Somebody else needs changing
    — Personal change
    — No cure—just how he/she is and always will be

Instilling doubt

Instilling doubt is a procedure or technique that works better when joined with a commitment to change as a matter of faith. Practitioners subtly cast doubt on the validity of the family's current system of interaction. The presenting problem seemingly demonstrates the difficulty is unresolved within the current belief system and with the behavioral interaction patterns as they now exist. During initial sessions, instilling doubt is introduced into the therapeutic process to ensure the participants are willing to make the necessary effort to change what they believe in what they think they know or perceive to be the problem.

Four directive components of therapy (see figure 6.5) need to be established early in the treatment plan and process. Commitment to each component must be obtained and responsibility accepted in the first session before proceeding with therapy. Otherwise, the treatment plan will fail.

Figure 6.5. Directive components of therapy		
Commitment		**Practitioner statement**
1.	At least two participants need to express a willingness to change.	"I will work with you (to remove the presenting problem) if you will do what I ask."
2.	If there is a parental problem, parents must first assume the responsibility for changes.	"You must assume greater responsibility for changing the presenting problem if genuine change is expected."
3.	Explicit effort is necessary. There are no quick fixes.	"All rules should be consistent and apply to all members of the family. All members are subject to consequences of their behavior."
4.	The consequences of not changing will be explicit.	"The presenting problem may improve, but other problems might develop."

Pattern changes

The overarching purpose for family therapy lies in altering the context and to remove what is hampering change. Practitioners change basic behavior patterns by manipulating the perspective driving the behavior causing the problem. They facilitate changes in the patterns of behavior associated with the presenting problem. The goal is to remove the presenting problem and decide what is necessary to shift the belief structure and allow the desired behavior to occur.

The individual or family unit given tasks and coaxed into working toward smaller goals and positive functional behavior patterns along with an altered family belief structure based on the therapeutic casting of doubts onto existing beliefs (*e.g.*, "This is what you have been doing and now I am going to cast doubt on whether you should continue to do it or not").

TASK SETTING

<u>In-session</u> opportunities occur when verbal statements create a slightly different perspective or when an assigned task forces the family to interact differently during therapy. Practitioners identify and select tasks after asking questions that may include parental negotiation or determination of consequences for misbehavior. These tasks force new interactions around the presenting problem and may occur in-session or out-of-session. Both completed and uncompleted tasks are assessed.

<u>Out-of-session tasks</u> are usually called *homework assignments*. Tasks that require specific changes in behavioral interactions outside of therapy are a hallmark of many strategic and behavior therapies (*e.g.*, journaling as part of cognitive behavioral therapy) and can be a valuable source of information for the practitioner. Out-of-session tasks require interactions that need guidance for completion, time and opportunity, and specific situations to consider.

Tasks should not be assigned without a specific reason. Change comes not from the task, but from the quality of the therapeutic relationship that permits a perspective shift in the participant and family unit or system. In some cases, no task needs to be given. In other situations, practitioners may give a task at each session. Whether or not to assign a task depends on the treatment plan, what the practitioner determines the participants need, and the level of compliance expected.

Assignments

Assignments can be either written or oral. Behavior-oriented family practitioners are prone to assign written tasks, such as journaling. Non-behavior-oriented therapists seldom request written tasks. Written contracts or agreements are especially helpful, for example, for single parents who have abdicated their parenting responsibilities in exchange for their child's friendship (*i.e.*, parentification).

Behavioral family practitioners document and detail reciprocal actions among the family members and push for their acknowledgment of complicity in the presenting or actual problem. To successfully implement a family contract or agreement, all family members must agree to change their behavior—which is the overarching objective of family therapy.

Written tasks rely on specifics, while verbal (or oral) tasks tend to be more general. Written tasks utilize greater specificity of action and reaction; whereas, verbal tasks depend more on the assumed internal capacity of the individual family members to respond appropriately when given the opportunity. For example, a father might be asked to make sure his children are in their bedrooms by 9 pm each night, providing him with an opportunity to become more responsible. This is a verbal assignment (or oral contract or agreement) requiring no corresponding written assignment.

Compliance

Practitioners should only require a task that has a strong potential for being successful. This will encourage greater compliance by family members as the therapy progresses. Tasks and techniques serve as vehicles for change. The impetus for change comes from the therapeutic process and practitioners' interpersonal interactions with participants within the family system.

Caution: Too often, self-help and professional books, videotapes, and workshops make it appear they are the stimulus for changed behavior. They are not. These evidence-based therapies are effective resources only for providing information and opportunities for new behaviors to be identified and addressed conjointly with ongoing professional therapy.

PUTTING IT ALL TOGETHER IN SESSION

Let us first understand the facts, and then we may seek the cause. -Aristotle

Now that the treatment plan, NEG methodology, therapeutic process, and some tools have all been gathered, what might an actual session look like? It begins with the first contact. YOU are the interactional faith-based family therapy practitioner.

First contact

The initial contact generally comes by phone. Location and fees are discussed. Everyone relevant to the presenting problem is requested to be at the first session, including all adults and children in the family unit. However, if not everyone is able to come to the first session, get all the participants you can to attend.

Aside from completing any intake forms and paperwork you require, the first contact is an opportunity to frame the treatment expectations based on the assumption that family problems are related to the entire family, not solely to an identified person (IP) within the family unit. Avoid accepting or making any indication of causality during the first contact. As you discuss the expectations for a treatment plan for family therapy, do NOT imply the family or any particular family member caused the presenting problem—suggest only that the whole family is necessary to fix the problem.

Who is present in the session?

Consider shuffling people in and out of the therapy room at times. Remember, you need only those family members (or relevant members of the system) who provide leverage to alter the interactions or behaviors that need changing.

First session objectives

The following objectives are usually addressed during the first session with your participants:

1. Join with the family and slowly gather verbal and nonverbal information.

2. Assume that current family interactions define the family system (language usage, beliefs, myths, rituals, perspectives).

3. Assess the presenting problem, remembering this may not be the actual problem.

4. Determine limitations and pace of the therapeutic process.

5. Choose only an initial task that is sure to be absolutely successful and will allow new behavior to be integrated into the treatment plan.

Once you have completed your first session, review the information you acquired from the participants and begin to plan for subsequent sessions and how they might unfold.

Subsequent sessions

There are no prescribed procedures for what to do in any given session. The goal for each session is simply to guide the participants to evaluate and willingly change faulty mental maps and problematic behaviors. The original presenting problem may shift in subsequent sessions as participants gain more understanding of their roles in the dysfunctional patterns and broken familial relationships. Each therapeutic maneuver should be goal-directed, attempting to alter a pattern, gain a perspective, or remove a presenting problem.

The following is an example of altering a pattern while shifting a problem away from a dysfunctional behavior using sequential questioning:

You (therapist) to father: Has Johnny's behavior reached an almost intolerable level?

Father: Yes.

You: Will it continue to get worse if something does not change?

Father: Yes.

You: Do you want it to stop?

Father: Of course!

You (slowly): Do you want it to stop badly enough to change the way you talk to him about your ex-wife and your son's mother?

Sequential questioning is a term for the use of a series of interrelated, predetermined questions in response to the participant. The conversation moves in the opposite direction of where the participant or family member expects to go. The above scenario tells the father you want him to appreciate his contribution to his son's behavior problem, which may be a paradigm shift for the father.

Metaphors (*i.e.*, figures of speech where a word or phrase is applied to an object or action that is representative of something else) are also important techniques to help you teach, induce a perspective (or paradigm) shift, and facilitate changes in behavior. People suspend normal critical evaluation and absorb the message of the metaphor without concern for detail or defensiveness. You, as the practitioner, must have the confidence to use sequential questioning and metaphors comfortably to be effective with the process. Confidence comes from repetition as you gain experience in working with participants and managing your process.

Documentation

Documentation is generally for your benefit as a professional practitioner. It is a way of maintaining records or notes of sessions for future reference or to assure continuity of therapy from session to session. Some institutions may require a certain amount of record-keeping on any participants or family members being cared for there, *e.g.*, those who are hospitalized briefly for medication therapy. You need to be aware of such a possibility. If you as an interactional faith-based family therapist has participants in such institutions, you must be sure to become familiar with the related policies regarding documentation and comply accordingly.

In private practice, however, formal documentation is usually expected by State Regulation Boards, especially for licensure and credentialing and to meet any legal and ethical requirements. The best forms of documentation include an informed consent for keeping the work with participants and family units, practitioners, and the rule of law in your state or county clearly specified and protected.

Termination

When therapy is done properly, the individual participants or family members complete the process with the presenting/actual problem under control and an inherent belief they can handle future situations and problems. Problems are viewed in terms of making shifts of perspective with competence and confidence, so they are overt and manageable rather than covert and beyond control. Instilling the idea that the family members knew all along what was needed is critical for them to be able to own the changes in their mental maps and behavior patterns. At termination, then, your therapy has been successful if the following occurs:

Family members have moved beyond how they viewed their problems prior to treatment and now express confidence in their ability to handle future situations;

They do not assume it was merely you or your ability as their therapist that changed their situation, perspective, or behavior patterns; and,

They recognize God has given them a healthy outpouring of His special grace as they draw upon their faith and their connectedness to one another in meeting life's challenges and triumphs.

Failures

Failures do occur. Another form of treatment rather than interactional faith-based family therapy may be more effective in some cases, especially those requiring medical treatments. Your goal as the therapist is to minimize failures by learning from mistakes and by setting increasingly realistic goals for families based on their ability and willingness to change. Therapy tends to fail when the practitioner:

1. Holds to both the individual and the deficit models of family therapy and attempts to use both approaches in the same way;

2. Demands change in behavior patterns without using the language of interaction;

3. Cannot "join the family" in the process;

4. Does not demand change or non-change;

5. Forces a task be completed despite contrary information given by the family;

6. Does not project a sense of artistry and creativity, *e.g.*, in negotiating expectations;

7. Does not manage or provide a sense of direction in therapy;

8. Fails to use humor or to listen to the verbal and nonverbal messages of participants

9. Is perceived as not being real or genuine by the participants; or,

10. Leaves participants without hope or the sense that ultimately God is in control, even though they must manage their own lives and behaviors.

Failure can be positive, as well, when it is used as a lesson builder and stepping stone to humility and improvement. Your beliefs in God—or your lack of belief—shapes the way you care about others and how you will practice interactive faith-based family therapy.

IN CONCLUSION

Preparing for interactional faith-based family therapy is an often long and arduous job. It requires commitment and careful, accurate, attention to treatment planning and doing therapy. Let's take a brief look at just some of what we have learned in these first six chapters.

In this and the earlier chapters of Part 1, we explored the historical and ahistorical development of interactional family therapy and faith-based practices. We went deeper into presenting problems, considered some perspectives of theory and technique, and explored the roles of participants and practitioners in faith-based counseling and therapy. Functions and interactional questions, important tools for assessing behavior and discussing changes, were presented. A theology of therapy and an overview of ethical practices provided a firm foundation for building a strong faith-based practice. Finally, we closed out Part 1 by diving into the strategies and approaches for planning and implementing treatment and doing therapy.

In part 2, we will look at guidelines and tools for the advanced practitioner, *e.g.*, further development of the NEG model, control and management, individual and couples issues, and children and adolescents. We also include outcomes and recommendations from focus groups with lessons learned and ideas for advancing concept analysis and care strategies. So, take a deep breath and let's move on!

PART II.

Interactional Faith-Based Family Therapy—Advanced Practice

We are all faced with a series of great opportunities brilliantly disguised as impossible situations…. The secret of living a life of excellence is merely a matter of thinking thoughts of excellence. Really, it's a matter of programming our minds with the kind of information that will set us free.
-Charles R. Swindoll

Advanced practice calls for further specialization in the general areas of interactional faith-based family therapy and practice. Practitioners use guidelines and tools to:

- Collect data;

- Assess situations, motivations, mental maps and beliefs, behaviors, and family systems;

- Plan an approach to treatment;

- Establish needs, expectations, and goals of participants;

- Evaluate and communicate progress; and,

- Terminate the therapeutic relationship.

In Part 2, we continue building on the theories and resources introduced in Part 1. We will look more closely at the NEG model, the roles of control and management within familial and therapeutic relationships, and briefly explore issues unique to individuals, couples, children, and adolescents in family systems wherein dysfunction has been assigned to one or more of the participants by the other family members. Presenting problems bring them into therapy. Practitioners use these problems to plan reframes, to better understand any resistance encountered during sessions and in completing tasks, and to develop a paradox to move the therapy forward when needed.

Sometimes, like Winston Churchill, a *paraprosdokian* statement can be added to the conversation to help participants relax and enter into the process or to introduce a paradox. A *paraprosdokian* (Greek, beyond expectation) is a figure of speech in which the latter part of a sentence, phrase, or larger statement is surprising or unexpected in such a way that it shifts the meaning. This usually occurs with an abrupt change of direction at the end, causing the participant or family to reframe or reinterpret their thinking in the moment. The reversed anticlimax it produces can disrupt silence, anger, or other behaviors that might be impeding therapeutic progress. A few examples from Monty Pelerin's World (2019) can bring a bit of humor in truth to the session:

- If I agreed with you, we would both be wrong.
- We never really grow up. We only learn how to act in public.
- I didn't say it was your fault. I said I was blaming you.
- I used to be indecisive, but now I'm not so sure.
- A clear conscience is usually the sign of a bad memory.
- Change is inevitable, except from a vending machine.
- I thought I wanted a career; turns out I just needed paychecks.
- Always borrow money from a pessimist. He won't expect it back.

- Going to church doesn't make you a Christian any more than standing in a garage makes you a car.

These last three chapters are designed to help family practitioners advance their work in faith-based therapy by examining and applying the best techniques for doing interactional therapy. This necessitates going beyond current methods

- To maximize what already exists,
- To identify what currently goes on between family members, and
- To adjust for the fulfillment of needs, expectations, and goals of families.

Traditional paths to psychotherapy and counseling set up processes to legislate practices. This entailed having individuals obtain state and sometimes federal credentials and licenses before being approved to practice. Regulating agencies held to historical boundaries of psychology to validate current educational requirements for mental health care and family practice professionals. However, practitioners are now exploring new, ahistorical paths as innovative paradigms are introduced and paradoxes and *paraprosdokians* are more than humorous breaks in the conversation. Spirituality and faith have become consistent therapeutic factors when working with individuals, couples, children, and family units. They are of particular interest to faith-based family therapists.

Finding common ground for working together is the first step in effective ahistorical interactional faith-based family therapy. The qualitative outcomes, and recommendations from focus groups in the last chapter of Part 2 with lessons learned and ideas for advancing concept analysis and care strategies offer insights into how practitioners can achieve that first step toward achieving intended goals, healing faulty mental maps and dysfunctional behaviors, and facilitating restoration of familial relationships when working with families and people of faith.

CHAPTER 7:
Putting Faith-Based Therapy in Perspective

You can't go back and change the beginning, but you can start where you are and change the ending. -C. S. Lewis

People are ready for therapy when they want to discover what to do instead of being told what to do about the seeming failures, challenges, and dysfunctions in their lives that impact their relationships. When they arrive, it is critical practitioners spend the first session getting to know the participants, identifying their perceptions of the problems they are facing, and establishing a therapeutic relationship with them. Remember, knowing *the person is more important than the theory* and respecting that reality is the first step in effective counseling or therapy, which is indeed more art than science.

Trial-and-learn is often how practitioners gain the ability to change, question, and find more effective ways to do faith-based family therapy. Many times they begin by first discovering what does not work and learning how to fail forward (Maxwell, 2000) as they grow in knowledge and wisdom. This is especially important in that it is also a skill they will want to teach their participants and family members. Consider what is meant by failing forward as a positive and necessary skill for practitioners and an asset for participants in therapy.

My great concern is not whether you have failed, but whether you are content with your failure. -Abraham Lincoln

To paraphrase Maxwell (2000), the difference between average practitioners and achieving practitioners is their perception of and response to failure and how they view mistakes. What is the difference and why is that important? Because no matter how difficult decisions are or how many mistakes occur, the key to overcoming them lies not in changing circumstances but in changing how practitioners and participants respond to them and internalize new ways of thinking (new mental maps) about failure as grounded in trial-and-learn opportunities when failing forward instead of stagnating as trial-and-error disappointments when failing backward (see figure 7.1). Mistakes must be acceptable and managed positively before anyone can learn from them and move on to make any genuine or lasting changes in how they interact with one another to deal with faulty mental maps or dysfunctional behaviors or to restore broken relationships.

Figure 7.1. Comparing failure: Backward and forward		
Failing backward (trial-and-error)	Blaming others Repeating the same mistakes Expecting never to fail again Accepting tradition blindly	Being limited by past mistakes Thinking I am a failure Quitting
Failing forward (trial-and-learn)	Taking responsibility Learning from each mistake Knowing failure is a part of progress Challenging outdated assumptions	Taking new risks Believing something did not work Persevering
Source: Maxwell, J. C. (2000). *Failing forward: Turning mistakes into stepping stones for success.* Nashville, TN: Thomas Nelson, Inc.		

The NEG model (Needs-Expectations-Goals) delineated in chapter 6 describes a normative process that people may dismiss, ignore, or avoid when attempting to engage in healthy familial relationships. Briefly, this therapeutic approach moves beyond traditional approaches to clarify that which is real and subject to real time for participants. As we move further into the implementation of therapy based on the NEG model, we find techniques and interventions for managing relationships as opposed to controlling them. First, practitioners guide participants in expressing *needs* by clarifying them without negotiating them. Then identify *expectations* by negotiating what others perceive as their own needs combined and stating what is an actual negotiated expectation. Finally, *goals* can then be developed, applied, measured, evaluated, and extended or changed.

By the end of the interactional faith-based family therapeutic process using the NEG model, practitioners expect the *presenting problem*, which initially brought the family into counseling or therapy, will have disappeared because reality and clarity are now accepted by the participants as legitimate. At this point, they will have realized that what is really occurring among the family members reveals the actual problem with a functional focal point. The goal is not to get rid of problems or to fix them but to make them realistic rather than allowing them to remain spiritually or emotionally confused.

All get what they want; they do not always like it.... God intends to give us what we need, not what we now think we want. -C.S. Lewis

The concept of *oneness* (allows uniqueness and individuality that are relational and manageable) is not always operational, nor does it always replace the concept of *sameness* (conformity and co-dependence that are competitive and controlling). Sometimes a radical decision must be made—yes or no—to facilitate real change. Someone might say, "I don't know why, but I'm not going to put up with this behavior anymore." What he/she is saying is, "I am not going to be controlled by that kind of behavior anymore because I have another option."

Emphatic behavior change (or *structured change*) becomes apparent by moving systematically through the NEG process with participants. This technique provides a guided outline for a treatment plan and opportunities to use effective interventions during sessions. To ensure constructive progress toward the intended outcomes for therapy, the final session needs to include at least two participants besides the practitioner. Each person present needs to hear what the therapist says to the other to prevent misunderstanding or misinterpretation of the practitioner's summary of the treatment plan, evaluation of the therapeutic process, and final comments and instructions.

A Paradoxical Pragmatic approach is prompted *only* when clarity is needed from another perspective. The Paradox inflates and distorts to the point it causes the brain to reboot and realign mental maps, causing the participant's relationship to move toward a chosen reality. A lack of epistemological change relating knowledge as distinct between belief and opinion, as well as modifications of behavior in the NEG process discussed in chapter 5, calls for a pragmatic reframing containing the spiritual and faith-based perspective.

Essentially, the advanced NEG model is a natural process slowed down long enough to identify boundaries (needs), develop effective communication (expectations), and gain perspective (goals) from a Paradoxical Pragmatic approach. The artistic implementation of planned interventions leads to clarification of personal and familial values and opportunities for change using techniques and maneuvers that challenge and redevelop the basic approach of interactive faith-based family therapy by enhancing the faith and spiritual clarity from what is unnecessary for a healthy relationship.

Black and Gregersen (2008) recommend the ARCTIC approach (figure 7.2) for describing major categories and sub-dimensions of needs people experience motivationally that are expressed in how families make decisions and manage functional and dysfunctional behaviors relative to their perspectives and perceptions of what is occurring within the family.

CATEGORIES	SUB-DIMENSIONS	EXAMPLES FOR PRACTITIONERS
Achievement	**Accomplishments.** NEED to meet or beat GOALS, to do better in future than how one did in the past	Families identify achievable goals for improving mental maps and dysfunctional behaviors
	Competition. NEED to compare one's performance with that of others and do better than they do	Family members often compare the thinking and behaviors of the identified person (IP) to those of others when deciding what is functional or dysfunctional behaviors or flawed mental maps
Relations	**Approval.** NEED to be appreciated and recognized by others	Individuals and family members seek approval by those within the family and others (*e.g.*, employers, clergy, family therapy practitioners)
	Belonging. NEED to feel a part of and accepted by the group	Individuals need to experience connectedness and belonging within the family unit; dysfunctional behaviors are often ways of reaching out to others when functional behaviors are not enough
Conceptual/ Thinking	**Problem solving.** NEED to confront problems and create answers	Families with difficulty in identifying problems accurately struggle to create effective solutions to situations and perceived aberrant behaviors from those within the family unit
	Coordination. NEED to relate pieces and integrate them into a whole	Families often become uncomfortable and disconnected when individuals are unable to relate to one another or experience one another as a unit, or system, of integrated members

Figure 7.2. ARCTIC approach to categories of needs

Improvement	**Growth.** NEED to feel continued improvement and growth as a person, not just improved behaviors	Many perceived dysfunctions in behavior are connected to flawed mental maps that determine how problems will be solved and what is or is not acceptable behavior within the family unit; no growth can occur until these are in alignment with one another and behaviors reflect acceptable family norms or traditions
	Exploration. NEED to move into unknown territory for discovery	Parent-child relationships may become tense or broken as children mature and begin to explore new ideas and behaviors troubling to their parents, *e.g.*, during adolescence and young adulthood
Control	**Competence.** NEED to feel personally ca-pable and competent	IPs may be described in marginalizing or demoralizing terms, *e.g.*, aberrant behaviors, incompetence, or erratic think-ing, that often leads to feelings of inadequacy, a sense of personal failure, and an inability to meet their own expectations or those of family members and others
	Influence. NEED to influence others' opinions and actions	This may be reflected in behaviors connected to families' attempts to conform to one another, to peers, or to those in authority, *e.g.*, family members may seek to impress therapists to influence their opinion of an IP or the family unit as a whole

Source: Black, J.S., & Gregersen, H.B. (2008). *It starts with one: Changing individuals changes organizations.* Upper Saddle River, NJ: Prentice Hall Pearson Education, Inc.

Practitioners may consider these ARCTIC categories and sub-dimensions of participant(s) needs: (a) when exploring needs, expectations, and goals expressed in how individuals and families control and manage decisions; (b) when determining what and how to address presenting and dysfunctional problems functionally; and, (c) when introducing and negotiating change while guiding healthy perspectives and perceptions within the individual and the family unit.

CONTROL AND MANAGEMENT

The primary dynamic in considering how to make decisions in faith-based family therapy is folded into a control-and-manage dyad. Understanding the differences in how this dynamic works in relationships is basic to achieving healthy outcomes in interactional communication. In working with families, the distinctions between these concepts lie in how they are represented in two tenets of humanity:

1. Who is in control or has ultimate control of self and others in life

2. How do individuals and families manage their relationships

Control: ...which He will bring about at the proper time—He who is the blessed and only Sovereign, the King of kings and Lord of lords.
(1 Timothy 6.15)

Management: Nevertheless, each individual among you also is to love his own wife even as himself, and the wife must see to it that she respects her husband. (Ephesians 5.33)

Families need these distinct differences in their experiences and situations for controlling life and its circumstances and those abilities to collaborate and manage issues. Within the human heart resides a desire to control circumstances, situations, behaviors, thoughts and ideas, self and others, even life and death. People are uncomfortable when they experience loss of control or overwhelming demands and perceived or real obligations in themselves or others.

Families establish fluid hierarchies of control and management within their systems that fluctuate as relationships ebb and flow across generations. The child today matures and becomes the caregiver for aging parents. Husbands and wives are partners who may exchange roles and responsibilities as situations and circumstances demand, *e.g.*, during child-rearing years and into retirement. They negotiate who controls and who manages finances, who will be the disciplinarian and who will be the support when corrections are needed, and who makes the final decision when there are multiple options available, sometimes exchanging roles and responsibilities to bring balance and boundaries into their spousal and parenting activities.

However, battling for control within the family system is a common pastime for many couples and family members, regardless of whether they are conscious or not of their behaviors or the mental maps that drive them. People who need to control are easy to identify—they frequently make demands, issue ultimatums, and demand obedience from others often without question. They may do this through verbal and nonverbal behaviors that are assertive, aggressive, passive-aggressive, or passive, *e.g.*, avoidance or silence, which contribute to establishing or maintaining control of situations, events, behaviors, thoughts, and other people. Avoidance and survival responses are subsets of controlling behaviors; they are not managing behaviors. For example, the need to evade unpleasant situations due to embarrassment or pain may result in attempts to control those situations through avoidance or silence.

Usually, when an individual engages primarily in controlling responses, the number of choices remaining or available is reduced to two or less, such as *pain* or *no pain*. Sometimes these reductionistic selections are oppositional, *e.g.*, black or white, good or bad, up or down, push or pull, reducing complex emotions and behaviors to simplistic determinants affecting the outcome of those options. Choice is relegated to an either/or constraint with control being the goal. When three or more options are available, choices and any potential consequences require management rather than control.

CASE STUDY:
Controlling an untenable situation

A woman lived in Washington state with her four children and a very difficult husband. One day, she simply dropped out of sight. Her family was greatly upset after a week had passed with no word from her. They could think of no reason for her to just disappear. After the first week, they filed a Missing Persons report with the local police department. When she had been gone for two full weeks, she called to tell her husband and her family she was in Hawaii, expressed her remorse for leaving them so impulsively, and asked if she could come home. Her husband said yes and invited her to return. However, instead of rejoicing that she was safe and returning to them, he was angry and insisted she stay at her parents' house rather than at home with him and the children. Each day she was required to drive to where the family lived some miles away. Her husband directed her to get the children out of bed, fix them breakfast, send them to school, clean the house, meet the children after school, fix them dinner, put them in bed, and return to her parents' house for the night.

After complying with these punishing constraints for two weeks, she made an appointment and entered faith-based family therapy. When asked why she had dropped everything and left for Hawaii, she replied, "I had two choices. I could have jumped off the bridge in Washington or escaped to Hawaii. Which one would you have chosen?" The therapist replied, "I would have chosen Hawaii, as well". The forlorn woman had been responding to her situation in "survivor mode". She was unable to perceive or identify any alternatives beyond her immediate survival. She convinced herself she had no other options and was trapped in an untenable position from which she had to escape, even if temporarily. She sought to control her situation by removing herself from it, unable to conceive of any way to manage her circumstances in the moment.

A managing approach to circumstances and situations requires three or more options, whereas a controlling one allows only for two or less choices. It is important to recognize the difference in these approaches for both are necessary at times. For example, it is critical to control a situation when there is a threat to the safety of the individual or family members. If you are driving your family car down the middle lane of a freeway and an 18-wheeler truck is bearing down on you from behind, what do you do? Do you look for three or more options or just get out of the way? You take control of the situation and move your vehicle out of the way to avoid a potential collision. Sometimes, it is necessary to take control during an emergency or when no one else is willing or able to make a critical or immediate decision. When there is no time to convince people to cooperate in or during an urgent or looming crisis event, control the situation and manage the discussion with family members afterwards around options for how best to respond next time.

How does this work in family systems? A key perspective around control and management in family systems is this: manage relationships or control people.

- Manage relationships to achieve <u>oneness</u>
- Control people for to acquire or maintain <u>sameness</u>

For example, if participants control for sameness and manage for oneness and if marriage is identified as a oneness concept spiritually, why aim at sameness as an objective for any marriage or familial relationship? What might that look like? Consider the military family system.

In the military it is important for those who serve their country to do a good job, usually through control and directive behaviors. Where they serve, though, makes a difference to how they are received by their spouses and family members. When soldiers are not deployed (*i.e.*, sent into duty outside of their homes to various other locations or countries) and go home at night to be with their families, they often experience a different response to their military bearing from their families. Family members are usually not impressed with rank or position. If those soldiers are commissioned officers, these high-ranking soldiers do not have an assigned parking place at home, and no one salutes them. Family members do not have the same military mission and are not interested in sameness with the soldiers in their midst. Why? Because the family is interested in <u>oneness</u>, which must be managed. They are not interested in sameness to be commanded, dictated, or controlled.

Control is most prominently implemented when raising children. When children are born and from infancy until approximately the age of ten years, parents generally have complete control over their children—what they eat, when and where they sleep, what they wear, who they interact with, where they go, what they learn, and so on. Preparing and teaching children continues to progress and advance towards the time when they become responsibly independent during late adolescence and early adulthood. During this time, control is exchanged for management and influence. Continuing to control children at this stage in their development may lead to overt or covert rebellion, emotional enmeshment in which boundaries are permeable or unclear, and in some cases, extended dependence on parents for decisions and support that cripples their ability to engage as independent adults on various levels.

Control behaviors frequently reveal control issues and behaviors in adolescents transitioning to young adults which are seemingly beyond control and are rarely effective, *i.e.*, ultimatums and demands. These behaviors often result in constant and consistent rebellion against such continued parental control that can seriously undermine or even destroy family relationships and interfere with children's healthy emergence into mature adulthood.

Much like the military all organizational systems have an underlying control agenda: businesses, governments, and schools, along with churches and other institutions of faith. The only genuinely true management model resides within the family system, specifically within the marriage relationship, and reflected in parent-child relationships. This may be why God uses stories and similes for the family and marriage to describe His relationship with humanity from Genesis to Revelation. Images of the family unit, behaviors and blessings for husbands and wives, expectations for parents and children, loving and sacrificial marriages, and consequences of divorce are all themes found in Scripture that God uses to teach people how to live and thrive in oneness. It is how He connects human beings to Himself and to one another through relationship.

Practitioners in interactive faith-based family therapy facilitate change through faith, which is always managed and never controlled. The word *faith* is the action of the process that is placed in some<u>one</u> not in some<u>thing</u>. For example, Christians worship God in a church and among other people; they do not worship the church building. Similarly, participants would be best to worship God in a marriage relationship rather than worship the institution of marriage.

Goals define how outcomes to therapy are measured, whether the process was successful or otherwise. Did the family meet its goals for entering into faith-based family therapy? Did the practitioner achieve the outcomes intended during the sessions with participants? Goals can act as a litmus test for differentiating between a controlled system tactic and a management approach to relationship. When the word *goal* is used in a management perspective, participants encounter a different nuance.

The goal for tools used in management activities is to encourage practitioners and participants to possibly extend a goal or change it rather than accept a succeed-or-fail outcome. Although the marriage relationship as expressed in our current society is often surrounded by institutions driven by demands for control by participants, marriage remains the single venue with pure management potential.

The Needs-Expectations-Goals (NEG) Model becomes actively stimulated in managed relationships. Neither of the authors has ever met anyone who having experience management in a relationship that depended on sharing a conjoint faith would consider returning to or accepting one that was embedded in a control model. When managing relationships through negotiated expectations and clarified needs to meet personal and combined goals, faith can always ground participants and their family members in caring and healthy responses to one another, moving them from dysfunctional to functional behaviors and thinking.

FUNCTIONAL AND DYSFUNCTIONAL

Essentially everything practitioners and participants might want to know about family counseling and therapy today can be found in books and accessed on computers. However, the key to successful family therapy lies in who is training others how to actually "do" counseling and therapy. If practitioners' approaches, processes, and outcomes are dysfunctional, the participants' results will be functional, as well. Many promoters of faith-based counseling and therapeutic techniques advocate what to practice instead of how to practice individual and family therapy. Generally, this focus on what rather than how leads to a *prescriptive* approach that becomes problematic as participants are often seen in generic, one-size-fits-all terms. In doing so, practitioners fail to address them as unique individuals and family units requiring their own therapeutic and faith deliberations.

In an age of information-only computers, knowledge becomes confused with wisdom. Using information wisely is a skill that is both caught and taught. The major differences reside in how and when knowledge is acquired, how it contributes to professional and personal growth, and how does it help practitioners and participants mature in wisdom and understanding. Knowledge is easy; wisdom is hard. *Knowledge* grows from facts, ideas, evidence, and data acquired through observation, research, and experience. *Wisdom* applies knowledge, lived experience, and action to create and build discernment about what is right and true, to determine and select accurate and just decisions, and to apply learning and knowledge to understanding and exploring healthy individual and family relationships.

To know wisdom and instruction, To discern the sayings of understanding, To receive instruction in wise behavior, Righteousness, justice and equity; To give prudence to the naïve, To the youth knowledge and discretion, A wise man will hear and increase in learning, And a man of understanding will acquire wise counsel, To understand a proverb and a figure, The words of the wise and their riddles. The fear of the LORD is the beginning of knowledge; Fools despise wisdom and instruction. (Proverbs 1.2-7)

Although most men are predominantly more <u>product</u>-oriented and most women are primarily <u>process</u>-oriented, technology tends to drive the one-answer-fits-all-people approach adopted by many counselors and therapists. Without true insight or understanding of the unique and varied nuances of individual and family needs, expectations, or goals, practitioners frequently advance a form of *philosophical uniformitarianism*, the idea that human beings act in the same way and with essentially the same mental maps in the past as they do in the present such that uniformity in practice will somehow bring about changed behavior in participants in the future.

However, this fallacious, prescriptive approach to family therapy provides few genuine answers to the myriad adjustment problems seen among individuals in family systems. The art of therapy blends knowledge and wisdom in seeking solutions with participants. How do practitioners prepare to engage with participants in the art of interactive faith-based family therapy, enabling families to move beyond the perceived and real problems that beset their dysfunctional members? This requires more than an information-only approach.

A similar limitation is true in faith-only counseling and therapy. When practitioners or participants assume that faith alone can meet all fluctuating and broken emotional needs, reduce psychological and physical distractions, and address every family's sociological expectations by presenting a theological dogma or doctrine into therapy, they are again practicing with a misleading and prescriptive singularity of purpose. Practitioners need training on how to practice therapeutically rather than being given scripts for what to say or how to advise families by repeating accepted clichés or scriptures or reiterating religious formulas for every presenting problem or dysfunctional behavior. The functional family knows how to be a family. The dysfunctional family has tried and failed and is now colliding with the consequences of that failure. They need more than platitudes and psychological prescriptions.

What is the difference between functional and dysfunctional? *Functional* is defined as something that is practical or useful in how it properly operates or works and has a special purpose or intent, activity, responsibility or task. In faith-based family therapy, "functional" refers to the thinking, behaviors, and roles of the individuals within the family system and whether or not each participant reflects the norms of the family unit. Are participants able to relate to one another and think and behave personally, spiritually, physically, and socially according to their agreed family principles and faith with mutual trust and respect even when they disagree? *Dysfunctional* thinking, behaviors, and roles are reflected in unhealthy activities, poor decision-making, impaired or disruptive behaviors, spiritual distress, and fractured or broken relationships between and among family members.

Faith-based family practitioners help participants understand the differences in knowledge and wisdom, the variances in functional and dysfunctional processes and behaviors, and how these concepts apply to their familial relationships. Negotiating and facilitating functional responses to painful or chaotic events, situations, relationships, and behaviors, for example, require practitioners and participants to expand and develop their understanding of personal needs, expectations, and goals. The statement "I need . . . so I can . . ." validates the underlying mental maps in play when needs are isolated so nothing else can be used as an excuse or crutch for behaviors when determining what is truly needed to exist or function effectively within the family system.

Needs quickly translate into values, the boundaries that keep individuals from compromising their integrity or overstepping personal and familial value systems. A need might be expressed as "I _need_ integrity in the way I make decisions, _so I can_ be consistent in how I answer others". No one could or would argue with that need as stated. However, to say "I _need_ rules and regulations, _so I can_ answer everyone in the same way" is actually a want. _Wants_ tend to establish or set up barriers, often building walls instead of identifying relational boundaries. Such _barriers_ serve to increasingly isolate people, allowing them to intentionally keep others at arm's length or even completely reject them from their lives.

Boundaries are the limitations created by individuals to ascertain reasonable, safe, and acceptable ways for others to behave towards them. Rules and guidelines defining those boundaries delineate how others can safely move toward and around one another and how they will respond when boundaries are breached. Personal boundaries are physical, emotional, spiritual, and mental limits people establish to protect themselves from being manipulated, used, or violated by others. They allow individuals to separate who they are, and what they think and feel, from the thoughts and feelings of others. These boundaries help people express themselves as unique individuals, while acknowledging the same in others (Hereford, n.d.).

Without boundaries, there is no safety. Recognizing and accepting boundaries as reflective of personal and familial value systems help inform needs. When a person states a need that reflects a value (*e.g.*, healthy behavior), it becomes a recognizable boundary; and, the subsequent response in maintaining or breaching that boundary becomes a rational choice for the participant. When no conjointly recognized needs have been identified or stated, the participant frequently erects barriers that may quickly fall when under pressure.

For example, a participant enjoys the company of a family member who smokes. The participant has health problems and is now struggling to quit smoking himself. Although he wants to spend time with his relative, he does not want to join him when he is smoking. While there is currently no barricade, a boundary related to his <u>need</u> to stop smoking <u>so he can</u> be healthy has been established. However, it can be breached if the relative insists on smoking when the participant is present or if he exerts pressure on him to "just have one cigarette—surely that won't hurt you..." or "just step outside with me while I smoke..." The participant may experience added stress if he believes he is being forced into a compromising situation where his personal boundaries and values are being compromised, where his <u>needs</u> are being disregarded. To avoid responding to the invitation to smoke or to be exposed to smoke, knowing it was bad for his health, but hesitating to disappoint his relative, the participant decided not to bend but keep his boundaries and values long before those circumstances occur by recognizing his need (or boundary) to stay committed to those values and suggesting other activities they could do together instead of smoking.

Just as individuals have needs, values, and appropriate boundaries, so do family units. When the practitioner sees these basic but critical principles are recognized, supported, and experienced within the context of a family system, that family is considered functional. Three models illustrate functional and dysfunctional behaviors found in most family systems. Two are dysfunctional; one is functional.

- Enmeshed model

- Rigid model

- Functional family model

These models—those most often seen by practitioners in family therapy—encompass transcultural and international patterns of behaviors and thinking experienced by most participants at some point in their familial relationships with one another (figure 7.3).

Figure 7.3: Three Family Models

FM 1. Enmeshed Family (Dysfunctional):

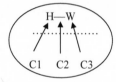

No roles modeled
No boundaries
<u>C</u>hildren have direct access to mother (<u>W</u>ife)
    or father (<u>H</u>usband)

FM 2. Rigid Family (Dysfunctional):

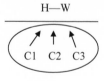

No roles modeled
Boundaries act as barriers
No direct contact with H-W relationship

FM 3. Functional Family:

H-W dyad modeled
Boundaries are visible
Visible relationships

    Note: Boundaries are not barriers. Barriers keep people away.
    Boundaries, needs, and values are often the same thing.

Enmeshed model

The *enmeshed model* is seen in family units when family members become caught up in repeating unhealthy and dysfunctional patterns, assuming inflexible roles in which family members become entangled with the one another, enabling disruptive and mutually damaging behaviors and relationships, and frequently inhibiting individuality and blurring boundaries among family members.

The family system is usually comprised of a father, a mother, and children. When there are few or no boundaries for parameters for roles and responsibilities between husbands and wives, a lack of autonomy and independence evolves, fracturing relationships. The children in these families may have access to their individual parents but without definitive, consistent, or cohesive structure, values, or boundaries. They have little comprehension of what adults or parents do, what responsibilities they have as a family, or how husbands or wives are supposed to interact with one another.

In an enmeshed family system, children may learn about sameness but do not learn the boundaries or potential for oneness in either the marriage dyad or in the family unit. Safe, healthy relational boundaries between husbands, wives, and children allow family members to have private lives separate from one another. For example, parents share confidences and intimacies with one another that are not shared with children or others outside of the family unit.

Rigid model

The *rigid model* establishes familial boundaries which are controlled and closed, isolating all members of the core family unit and not allowing outsiders in or out or making it difficult for others to interact with the family members. This dysfunctional structure that requires family members to think and behave in a prescribed manner to maintain the status quo. Although participants may recognize that change is inevitable, they resist any change or perceived interference from those outside the family unit. They may attempt to prevent others from changing, maturing, and eventually leaving the family unit. This is then extended to such isolation that others outside the family cannot join them, such as through dating or marriage. This closed system has a rigid boundary that may also discourage or reject those who leave the family unit from returning.

The family system of father, mother, and children is disengaged and generally does not tolerate collaborative contact with open boundaries or values in the husband-wife dyad. It does not support an interactional approach to marriage and family relationships. Family members operate among themselves with limited outside associations and ideas. For example, a family with a mentally handicapped child or one with a drug or alcohol addiction would try to manage the situation from home with no outside interference or help. Children with little or no parental collaboration may be restricted to home schools or familial learning groups rather than attending a community institution. The rigidity of family boundaries may be so tightly held that questions of a personal nature are projective or child-generated. Authority lines between parents and children are clear but often suffocating, negating the normative changes inherent in healthy relationships.

Disengaged families usually have a strong line of authority among family members with little communication, poor emotional expression or support, rigid boundaries, and dysfunctional spousal relationships, with one spouse being unyielding and controlling with the other being passive. These families rely heavily on rules and control without relationships. Children often express eagerness to reach adulthood and the ability to leave this family system.

Functional family model

The *functional family model* is an open system characterized by wholeness with each family member communicating with one another honestly and comfortably. Each participant gives input into family matters with parents making the final decisions for children's well-being. Husbands and wives often negotiate family decisions not already allocated to one or the other. Husbands and wives stand together in oneness, providing checks and balances to support purposeful family behaviors and healthy mental maps.

The functional family remains engaged with one another and with their communities. It is usually identified first by a strong, mutually supportive husband-and-wife dyad. The father-and-mother relationship is clearly represented in established adult roles, familial boundaries, and shared nurturing. The children recognize family responsibilities as family values and boundaries that are easily identifiable and respected. The husband-and-wife dyad combines oneness, belongingness, identity, faith, and responsibility within the context of the family relationships.

CASE STUDY:
Functional or dysfunctional family roles

A husband and wife are in counseling because they do not understand why their children married and later decided to divorce, causing them a great deal of pain as grandparents. When the children were young, the husband could not get a job that paid as well as his wife's job did. The wife focused all her energy on work and family, so her family could have an advantage financially. Her children, a boy and a girl, later sought out similar behavior patterns in their mates, emphasizing family first. However, the roles each family member played were confusing as to who nurtured, who modeled leadership, and who made the final decisions for the family. The communication was definitive and there was little negotiation or collaboration.

Assessment: The children were confused because the parental roles in their family system were unclear. The husband-and-wife issues were turned into a couple's issue with equitable responsibility problems rather than remaining individual responsibilities. This transition in familial roles and parental responsibilities may have caused the children confusion as adults when they attempted to identify their own functional responsibilities as participants in their marriages. The adult children did not understand that equality does not mean functionality in healthy relationships. Functional role clarity nearly always involves emotional, mental, and behavioral issues with healthy responses to events and situations, including marriage.

In a sense, dysfunctional, disengaged families arise from dysfunctional models rather than from dysfunctional, disengaged people. However, dysfunctional people tend to create and engage in dysfunctional relationships and marriages that are passed on to current and future generations. Moving participants from dysfunctional behaviors and faulty mental maps to functional relationships and healthy mental maps calls for changes in perceptions and perspectives.

PERCEPTION AND PERSPECTIVE

The key to doing effective interactional faith-based family therapy lies in introducing change so therapy gives *perspective*, another attitude or point of view, a way of visualizing concepts and relationships, adding height, depth, width, and distance or positionality. A philosophical paradigm shift resembles the kind of change introduced by the practitioner as artist. Like craftsmen working in their favorite media, practitioners implement therapeutic techniques that embody simplicity, parsimony, and integrity, thereby taking the therapy further forward for genuine, sustainable change to occur within the family system.

Perspective artfully draws on one's sense of proportion, balance, or symmetry to place events or situations relative to something else in the way they are mapped mentally. Perspective offers comparisons in ways of thinking about a problem or issue in a reasonable way that relies on knowledge and wisdom to resolve accurately. When reviewing family circumstances or events, it is important for the practitioner to investigate what each family member's perspective of those circumstances or events means. This validates the different roles each person might play in changing relationships within the family unit to become healthy and supportive of boundaries and values recognized by all family members within the family system.

Practitioners incorporate the art of subtle influence to facilitate changes in patterns of interactions between and among family members to facilitate change and appropriate self-confidence. They determine and modify the process as it unfolds within the sessions. Bowen (1978, 1993) introduced *family perspective* when he developed the *Family Gram* (or *genogram*), a diagrammatic chart outlining the family history—birth order, blended families, death, gender, liaisons, conflicts—to provide a visual perspective of how behavior patterns can develop and are influenced from generation to generation. Behavior patterns such as marriage, divorce, abuse, abortion, and suicide are detailed over several generations to provide insight into current patterns of behaviors within the family system.

When practitioners look at a presenting problem or issue from a different vantage point with a broader or narrower focus, they can accommodate change in relationships or behaviors as intentionally designed paradigm shifts. *Perceptions*—sometimes called *insight* or *intuition*—are the mental maps and impressions people have for understanding and interpreting behaviors, alter with more information. They do not have to be relational or require accuracy in their context or application to reality. Although perceptions can be corrected and stabilized by faith in or about something or someone, too often decisions are hastily made on too little evidence and relationships ended solely on erroneous perceptions.

Figure 7.4 Perspective, Perception to Reality

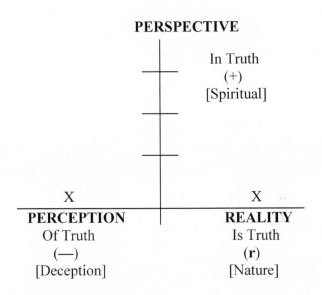

It is the *nature* of humanity to believe that *perception* could be *reality*. With *perspective*, *truth* becomes *spiritual* when scripture is used. In reality, perception deteriorates into *deception* without Truth. Moving from perception to reality and back is a linear process—in which most people participate each day of their whole lives—sometimes moment by moment—rather than recognize perspective as a mitigating factor in their decisions and reflected in their relationships. Perception as reality has become more and more absorbed by today's culture.

For example, an initial perception of a woman snapping commands and ordering people around becomes very different when the whole picture unfolds as the seemingly aggressive woman yells for someone to "Call 911! I think my husband's having a heart attack!" Another person steps forward and says that he is trained in CPR. The woman pulls back to give the rescuer room to help her husband. The perspectives of those who are observing begins a realign themselves in their thinking and their perspectives rapidly change. Instead of a loud, aggressive woman, they now see a frightened wife in need of comfort and support.

Questioning perception introduces perspective but does not validate family roles or explain behaviors. Perceptions do occasionally result in correct outcomes, such as when someone:

- Professes insight into another person's character based on his or her behavior,

- Experiences an intuition about a situation based on certain evidence, or

- "Has a hunch" about how an event might turn out.

Because perceptions are subjective ways of experiencing reality through the senses and interpreting the world through external stimuli and mental impressions, they are vulnerable to manipulation. Two members of the same family can look at a situation through the lens of their individual senses and argue vehemently with one another about the accuracy of each one's perception of that situation. When this occurs, the truth generally lies in both arguments and requires perspective to arrive at genuine understanding and consensual agreement about what actually happened and how they might respond together to manage the outcome.

Perceptions are generally benign until they coalesce into "group perception." They then become a shared belief, which is validated simply because multiple people agree with the stated group perception. Family therapy practitioners disrupt and manage perceptions in individuals and in family units to therapeutically intervene and facilitate healthy change rather than validate dysfunctional behaviors, misconceptions, or faulty mental maps of one or more family members.

Expanding perceptions into perspectives in faith-based family therapy requires practitioners to instill hope, which is demonstrated by their willingness to identify and advance the needed transitions within the family. The concepts of perception and of perspective in this process can be seen in the graphic urban legend of a naval ship entering strange waters without recognizing other ships in the area.

"THE PARADIGM SHIFT"
involving perceptions and perspectives

Cruising off the coast of an island, the ship's commander saw a light ahead. Perceiving he was about to encounter what appeared to be another vessel, he rapidly signaled a message, "CHANGE YOUR COURSE". The message came back, "YOU CHANGE YOUR COURSE." Believing they were on a collision course, the captain signaled back, "I <u>ORDER</u> YOU TO CHANGE <u>YOUR</u> COURSE". The signal again came back, "<u>YOU</u> WILL HAVE TO CHANGE <u>YOUR</u> COURSE." The commander angrily signaled, "THIS IS A UNITED STATES NAVY BATTLESHIP". And, a signal was sent back, "AND I AM A <u>LIGHTHOUSE</u>". A perception was replaced by a new perspective .

The Paradigm shift sometimes occurs when reality sets in and truth presents itself. The Captain in this story had another perspective; however, he rapidly corrected his previous perception and changed course, thereby saving his ship and those on board. Though it may have seemed the lighthouse keeper was deceiving the Captain by withholding important information until the last minute, both lost valuable time by not identifying themselves immediately and choosing instead to engage in a briefly deceptive power play with one another. *Deception*, the process of organizing thoughts and ideas by concealing or not considering other important facts, either knowingly or unknowingly, nearly led to a tragic outcome. If the captain had checked his nautical charts or asked a few questions, he might have recognized that the light emanated from a lighthouse. Conversely, if the lighthouse keeper had identified the lighthouse in the first response, the entire incident would never have occurred. When the perspective was finally introduced, everything shifted.

The greatest enemy of perception is deception. Acceptance of a single erroneous perception in a marriage that has been lost or cast aside may remain with the participants for the rest of their lives, embedded in a deceptive perception of whatever went wrong in their relationship based on their perspectives. Addressing such perceptions calls for a perspective of faith that validates the new perception, which offers participants unlimited opportunities to experience their faith in oneness. Faith is reflected in acceptance and forgiveness by something or someone greater than a perception of what happened and opens individuals to placing trust in a living God.

Reframing perception and perspective to shift paradigms

Remember the story of the grieving man and his disobedient, intrusive children in chapter 4? The man rode a train with his four children, who were disobedient and bothering other passengers. The man sat silently while his children ran wild throughout the train.

- Based on your initial perceptions, what would you expect the man to do about his children?

- You decide to confront the man. As you are speaking to the man, he tells you that his wife has just died. He and the children are returning from her funeral. What do you say now that the situation has been clarified giving another perspective?

- The man sadly explains that the children loved their mother very much. She died of a drug overdose. What are your thoughts at this point?

- The grieving husband went on to explain how his wife had been kidnapped and forced to take the drugs to which she became addicted. The man responsible is now in jail. What are you feeling? Any perception changes?

How many "paradigm shifts" or perspective changes did the woman in the story experience? As the practitioner walked them through the story, did the family members make any shifts in their perspectives about what was occurring on the train? Exploring perceptions and creating an accurate perspective are two of the most important therapeutic techniques in interactional faith-based family therapy.

IN CONCLUSION

The NEG model is a central approach to interactional faith-based family therapy for exploring the roles of control and management within familial and therapeutic relationships in family systems. Presenting problems and a need to address dysfunctional behaviors and faulty mental maps assigned to one or more of the participants by family members often bring families into therapy. Practitioners use these problems to plan reframes, to better understand any resistance encountered during sessions and in completing tasks, and to develop a paradox. These help participants recognize when control and management impact their relationships and move the therapy forward when needed to correct participants' perceptions and perspectives.

For many practitioners educated and grounded in historic and traditional psychotherapies, working with people of faith—or with families of multiple faith practices and beliefs—can be challenging and enlightening. When God enters the process, He impresses practitioners and participants with new mental maps, the maps carried in their heads that frame personal and professional views of what is right and wrong, healthy and unhealthy, good and bad, acceptable and unacceptable, ethical and just. Practitioners walk with participants through their identified problems, helping them to separate function from dysfunction in their behaviors and thinking, and realign their perceptions and perspectives with the realities of lived experiences within their family systems when they encounter challenges and opportunities to grow in faith and oneness.

CHAPTER 8:
Family Relationships

The compatibility of a couple and the quality of a relationship lies in the way they handle their arguments and differences. -Nishan Panwar

Although problems are often easier to manage if they are shared with others, there are some difficulties that are more individual-oriented issues than couple or family-specific issues. In the previous chapter, we reviewed control vs management processes and how they impact family systems. When one family member attempts to force an issue with or for another, tries to convince someone to explore, eliminate, or replace an identified concern, it may be seen as an attempt to control the individual, or identified person (IP), believed to "own the issue" or problem.

For example, if one partner is not satisfied sexually, he or she may make that problem a couple issue. One individual might say, "I want you to do this sexually" when the other person does not feel comfortable participating in the desired behavior. The request as stated may be interpreted as a form of manipulation such that the partner must conform now that the *individual* issue has become a *couple* issue. Personal ownership of the problem is removed when a sexual problem for one is reframed as an intimacy issue for both participants. However, if both partners accept the identified problem as a couple, it may be viewed as either a burden or a blessing but still manageable.

Generally, when an individual issue causes one person in a relationship to compromise individual integrity or to breach personal boundaries, thereby making him or her feel uncomfortable about his or her values related to that issue, the individual issue becomes a controlling one. The response usually indicates the compromising participant is not managing the event or situation and is attempting to make the individual issue a couple issue.

When an individual issue becomes a couple issue by default, it impacts the relationship negatively. At that point, participants may cease making individual decisions for themselves and retreat into a command-and-control relationship with one another, for example. When this occurs, conjointly controlling rather than managing the event or situation and merging this with an unclear individual issue or a couple issue, the actual problems become confusing and sometimes hidden.

Determining the difference between what is an individual issue and what is a couple issue can be complicated and fluid. In the previous example, sex began as the individual issue and intimacy the couple issue. However, an individual's sex issue may not affect the couple's intimacy issue. For women, sex is usually one of many factors of intimacy; for most men, sex appears to be a focused event which may or may not include intimacy. Without the ability to perform, sex and intimacy may become problematic for both participants. This example is a classic one in demonstrating one of the individual and couple issues that often drive participants to seek family counseling and therapy.

Assigning problems as individual or couple issues provides a perspective of areas and opportunities to consider for couple restoration and growth. This potentially steers participants away from the sameness that encroaches on many marriages, avoiding replicating areas of dysfunction that burden and disrupt so many family systems, and confronting uncertainty in individual and familial relationships.

Individual issues can cause one to compromise personal values. A husband who has experienced oral sex with another person convinces his wife that he needs—not wants—that kind of sex and she accommodates him. Later, she resents her husband and begins to mistrust him. She finds herself crossing a boundary she had set for herself and compromising her own integrity and health concerns because of an individual issue based on what he wanted of her. This behavior is a personal choice regardless of its perceived morality. However, other individual issues can also arise wherein she may develop a fear of HIV or other sexually transmitted diseases, a sense of spiritual or moral impropriety, or concern about his possible sexual activities outside of the marriage. Eventually these issues in the relationship begin demanding she modify more and more of what she accepts and feels comfortable with, stressing the marriage.

Such stressful situations are common in many marriages and family systems today. They play havoc on individual and couples' self-esteem, personal and marital pride, and individuals' sense of worthiness and ability to model acceptable behaviors behind closed doors and among family members. In the example, this individual issue became a couple issue that later returned to an individual issue extracting sacrifice and heightened control factors, a situation that often result in bitterness and anger. The desire to please a partner who commands behaviors that cause stress or unwanted compromise is not an expression of love. Instead, where these experiences are shared, they may evolve into a form of *capturing* and *conquering* behavior. Individual issues reflect one's values. As a couple are validated and balanced within the concept of oneness, their values, beliefs, and mental maps are reflected in their behaviors and relationships.

Sometimes people will attempt to push or "put on" other individual issues involving sex because of their own insecurities or fears. For example, a participant who was sexually molested as a child may come to an adult relationship with reasonable and negotiated expectations but still dealing with painful feelings about that early experience. How can a person face molestation and rape from the past and expect a partner to understand those issues if he or she had not experienced it, as well? However, discordant accusations such as "You don't know what it is like if you haven't been raped!" are hurtful and nonproductive. Ultimately, the only healthy shared part of this or any individual issue is what it can contribute to the couple: trust, faith, forgiveness, hope, and genuine oneness. Individual issues related to respect and trust, needs, expectations, and goals must be built over time for couple issues to achieve a oneness perspective.

We may have started as individuals, but now we are as one. -Bryon Pulsifer

Many individual issues are basic philosophical issues that affect lifestyle so there is little, if any, foundation upon which to build consistency or clarity. Typical individual issues might include a personal work ethic, going to bed early, or staying up late. For example, some people might feel more comfortable with partners who get up early and go to work at an office in a different location then where they live; whereas, others might favor not having regular office hours or a place to go and prefer to work whenever they felt they were at their best. Without adjustments to these individual issues, couple issues of sharing and occasional flexibility will not be resolved, affecting other couple issues and potentially resulting in relational problems.

Individual issues affect feelings and emotions. When participants use abstract terms—whether negative or positive—of *feeling trapped, smothered, isolated, invisible, lost, unappreciated, fearful, excited,* and similarly emotive depictions of their situations or relationships when expressing their issues, they are rarely communicated their needs clearly. Such subjective references are not concrete and often difficult to interpret accurately. Without greater clarity and more objective descriptors to help practitioners and participants understand individual issues, participants will not be able to accomplish genuine oneness in confronting the event or situation troubling them as a couple issue. When one partner in a marital relationship, for example, says "I love my spouse" and then has an affair with someone else, this individual issue negatively affects the couple issue of oneness and places the relationship in jeopardy.

Abstract, intangible terms frequently link emotions and feelings to fantasy rather than fact. The fantasy—an imaginative state of mind or incomplete mental map—leads to assumptions attempting to reach oneness. However, such abstractions and fantasies tend to result in perceived oneness that is only temporary or false. Genuine oneness needs the consistent testing of true devotion and responsibility over time to establish and anchor the relationship and couple issues.

[S]pirituality is not a religion. Spirituality has to do with experience; religion has to do with the conceptualization of that experience. Spirituality focuses on what happens in the heart; religion tries to codify and capture that experience in a system. -Thomas Legere

All individuals have spiritual beliefs with baselines expressed internally and within their relationships that allow oneness to be a couple issue and an individual issue. Every human being has three innate spiritual needs, regardless of how they express their beliefs and religious traditions (Carson & Koenig, 2008; Stoll, 1989). Broadly stated, they are:

1. The need for meaning and purpose

2. The need for forgiveness and hope

3. The need for connectedness and belonging

People of faith generally look to God to meet these needs as individual issues. They then bring these variable and continuing needs into their relationships, which become couple issues to be met and sustained through oneness at that point. If individual baselines are incongruent, couple oneness is difficult to achieve.

For example, many people of faith think simply belonging to the same church is all that is necessary for spiritual compatibility, often equating external behaviors with internal beliefs. However, confusion and disappointment ensue if they later discover differences in beliefs, traditions, and expressions of spiritual baselines resulting in a disconnect as individual issues collide with couple issues when participants seek to achieve oneness with one another. For example, one person might hold to a different spiritual baseline of forgiveness, acceptance, and grace applied to others, whereas the other person, *i.e.*, a significant other or spouse, might disagree, potentially creating a conflict in the relationship.

The wisdom of two people having to work at establishing oneness to experience such closeness in their relationship is consistent with practitioners identifying the motivation that comes from a faith-based approach to family therapy in exploring how participants think and live their lives in general. Understanding the uniqueness of marriage and the rationale of spiritual baselines, such as the meaning and purpose of belonging and acceptance, is important for individuals asking one another to be faithful and to commit to oneness in their relationships.

MEN AND WOMEN—TOGETHER?

For this reason a man will leave his father and mother and be united to his wife, and the two will become one flesh. -Matthew 19.5

The many blended and unique cultural ideologies today around gender differences and the more fluid relationships among men and women have significantly changed how practitioners approach therapy. Participants within marital relationships or family systems may present themselves in terms of an emotional gender than conflicts with their biological gender. When referring to men and women, male and female, husband and wife, *etc.*, within family systems, it has become increasingly difficult to identify genders using anatomical identifiers or references. However, *chromosomes,* the physical carriers of genes composed of DNA and associated proteins, and related biological differences remain objectively definitive in determining *male* or *female* in participants.

Faith-based family therapy practitioners work with participants based on their biological identifiers. Though some participants' gender-specific feelings may appear to be more flexible and less offensive to others struggling with sexual issues, their behaviors are generally linked to faulty mental maps in which they give precedence to emotions and feelings when subjectively defining or selecting a preferred gender identity. Whatever gender they choose, they tend to be convinced those who declare themselves to be a different gender—whether emotionally or physiologically—to be worlds apart from them in their thought processes and behavior patterns much of the time, further confusing already complicated relationships, especially for people of faith.

For relationships to be healthy, couples need to feel they impact their associations with one another positively and in partnership rather than controlling or being controlled by them. When someone feels genuinely connected to someone else, there can be mutual belongingness with spiritual and psychological growth and development in oneness. Pervasive *disconnection*, a form of spiritual distress related to unmet spiritual need, is frequently linked to depression, isolation, loneliness, and abandonment issues. Conversely, temporary or limited disconnectedness can drive individuals to seek out and join others in creating new relationships, renewing lost acquaintances, or establishing a community of fellowship, *e.g.*, with a church family. Similarly, such periods of disconnectedness might draw couples together, enabling them to eventually experience oneness. When expectations and boundaries are folded into this process and goals clearly identified, men and women (*i.e.*, males and females) together can achieve something life-changing with epistemological results grounded in new knowledge, justification, and the rationality of faith.

Regardless of how individuals self identify their gender, biological men and women carry unique mental maps and express themselves differently behaviorally. For example, women tend to reflect patterns of relational growth and expression, which are experienced more as a <u>process</u> rather than as a finished product. In a *process*, principles and beliefs are identified and responded to concurrently. For most females, reality and beliefs are by nature interconnected. In a sense, women integrate their values into what they consider to be "normal" to achieve mutually meaningful relationships with males.

On the other hand, men are usually more <u>product</u> oriented. The male culture tends toward questions like, "How bad will it be before it is over?" Fear of intimacy, loss of control, or cultural expectations can be of categorical concerns to men. It is more "let's fix it or get it done" more than "how did it get done". For example, males generally *do* sex and females *have* sex.

A relational paradox moves men to accept this basic urge to fix things, to focus on product outcomes, to compartmentalize issues ("everything has a time and a place"), while at the same time, driving them to connect to those who respond in process or developmental ways. A man may honestly decry, "I don't understand women!" Yet, a man of faith may quickly comprehend the message when God commands, "You husbands . . . live with your wives in an <u>understanding way</u> [emphasis added] . . ." (1 Peter 3.7) and attempt to understand his wife and the other females in his life.

Many men construe intimacy as sexual intercourse or some variation of it, *i.e.*, intimate physical contact. They often put wives, children, work, friends, church, school, and God into different mental categories or compartments, mapping them separately as unique units. To most men, intimacy is an event. Women, though, generally integrate and synthesize all aspects of their lives into complex events or complete processes. To a woman, intimacy is a relationship. For example, when a man makes love, he makes love to his significant other each time they are intimate. When a woman makes love, she makes love to her significant other, her husband, the father of her children, the defender of her heart and home, and sometimes, her spiritual leader. She folds him into her complete self within the context of who she is and who he is to her together in relationship with one another.

Generally, when men begin their lives, they experience a continual need to be significant to family and friends and to those with whom they work. They strive to establish a meaningful identity early in life. The most important response by others for a man is that he is respected for his abilities, qualities, or achievements as seen in how they treat him or react to his behaviors and decisions. Women often develop their identities through a process of personal growth, maintaining variations of that early identity at different places and times as they mature.

As a man ages, he seeks to accomplish whatever goals he has identified across the span of years, *i.e.*, education, work, or family goals. Frequently, he comes home with a gold retirement watch and settles into a more sedentary life, which often interferes with the woman who is continuing to advance her personal identity as she ages. This creates a disconnect that interrupts relationships and can result in dysfunctional behaviors and problematic mental maps that no longer fit the life unfolding in later years. Conjointly, sometimes the passion related to work, family, and spousal relationships may now be missing from both partners. The dynamism for meeting personal and family needs, negotiating collaborative expectations, and accomplishing fluctuating personal and professional goals in life that requires stimulation and abundant energy ebbs and flows differently for men and women individually and relationally across the life span.

This pattern is not new. It is clearly described in the Old Testament of the Bible. In Proverbs 31.10-31, the worthy woman, "an excellent wife", is presented in her many roles and responsibilities, *e.g.*, she goes to the marketplace, buys and sells property, manages hired help, maintains her household, cares for her family, helps the needy, and fears the Lord. Meanwhile, the "heart of her husband trusts in her" as the man sits in the gate, regaling others with stories of how great he is and what an important businessman and leader he is, and praises his wife "for her worth is far above jewels… and he will have no lack of gain" (vss 10-11). A similar pattern continues as, in his later years, men desire to enjoy what they worked for in life, telling their stories of work and war to friends and family alike (intimacy, familiarity, and closeness). Women seek new challenges, *e.g.*, learning, teaching, sharing, volunteering (identity, individuality, and uniqueness in person and ability). Men and women continue to process ongoing experiences and challenges in life with a different kind of "passion" than they embraced and accessed in their earlier years.

Exploring the differences between male and female genders can be humorous as well as serious. For example, Gray (2012) looked at how men and women communicate, express their emotional needs, and experience varied modes of behavior in his book *Men are from Mars, Women are from Venus*. The back cover declares, "Once upon a time Martians and Venusians met, fell in love, and had happy relationships together because they respected and accepted their differences. Then they came to Earth and amnesia set in: they forgot they were from different planets." The path to understanding gender differences between men and women is not limited to the exploration of any single gender. Rather, it is in the connectedness of two interacting individuals pursuing oneness and how their unique differences fit together physically, emotionally, socially, and spiritually. In the chaos and challenges of pleasure and pain of discovery and joining of men and women together, such are the joys and trials that cause the Spanish to say and the French to agree, ¡Viva la *diferencia!*

For the practitioner working through the complex interactions among males and females, the challenge is not in getting them to connect with one another but in getting them to stay connected. Taking advantage of normal relational curiosity in women and a need for self-assurance in men means treating most couples with attention to clarity needs, expectations, and goals as well as emotional timing.

CASE STUDY:
An affair to forgive -or- to divorce

A couple had been married for 30 years when the husband had an affair with someone he had met on the Internet. The couple once had two daughters. Their first daughter died from cancer during her senior year in high school. Their second daughter attended the same school, where she met and married a young man. Because the young man had attended the same faith-based school as their daughters, the parents were comfortable with their remaining daughter's choice.

While on their honeymoon, the young husband told his new wife that he did not want her contacting her parents again. They were now married, and he was in control of their decisions and relationships. The marriage was already in trouble. As they struggled and the wife became more isolated from her parents, she told them what her new husband had commanded of her. The wife's parents recommended counseling and referred them to their pastor. However, the situation did not improve in the young couple's marriage. A critical twist occurred when the pastor engaged in an affair with the young wife. This affair increased the tension in the marriage and eventually led to the pastor's dismissal from the church. Meanwhile, the daughter and her husband continued with marriage counseling for a number of years with a certified psychotherapist.

The tension remained and grew between the husband and wife. With all of the stress, the now wife-mother pulled further back emotionally from her husband-father. Through the years she turned inward to her faith and became involved in deepening her personal relationship with God. Over a long period of time, she found fulfillment and the support she needed in her faith. Conversely, her husband became more and more frustrated and angry with his wife and with God. Finally, after continuing for years in a steadily deteriorating marriage, he found someone on the Internet and made intimate contact with her, engaging in his own affair.

Now, 30 years in a troubled marriage have elapsed, and the couple wants to overcome their problems. The certified therapist was not successful in helping them heal their relationship. Do they now begin in the interactional faith-based therapy process?

Response

To determine the correct course of action for navigating the above problems, the interactional faith-based practitioner should first consider and analyze the following questions and responses:

- Has each spouse clarified his or her needs to one another with the help of the practitioner?
- Has the couple also negotiated their expectations and set their goals?
- If not, they will be talking divorce.

If proceeding, the practitioner begins with exploring where they <u>are now</u> and not where they <u>were</u> to plan and implement the faith-based therapeutic process.

Focus on relationship

The primary issue when working with men and women together in therapy is about how *people change rather than* why *they change.* Since relationships are so important in interactional faith-based family therapy, the problem of changing behavior and establishing a mutually acceptable familial structure must be addressed sometimes before pursuing resolution or restoration in relationships. This involves first overcoming the familiar and pre-set or embedded ideas of determining a specific reason or identified person believed to be responsible for the marital or familial dysfunction in the distant or recent past. Most resources available or referenced in many psychotherapy or self-help books, for example, for attaining immediate change generally support the individual rather than adapt, adjust, or change relationships. They speak to relational sameness rather than oneness.

Sameness or oneness, an example from the law

One way to look at the relational differences between sameness and oneness is through the lens of law. There is no crime in sameness or in the lack of *oneness* in relationships. The legal system is based on laws and principles considered to be moral, ethical, and legal. It does not require oneness; it essentially addresses only the principles of *sameness* and fair treatment, which work in law but are limiting in relationships. For example, if a problem lies within a person, the law expects that person can be fixed psychologically and behaviorally when supported by discipline and control through counseling or therapy. This is the legal rationale for court-ordered counseling and referrals for court-appointed psychiatric evaluations. It is not—nor should it be—within the purview of the law to judge a person's intent or ability to change.

Therefore, approaching counseling, psychoanalysis, and therapy as a quantitative or exact science is somewhat unrealistic and ineffective in achieving predictable behavioral outcomes or in helping men and women attain oneness with each other. The legal system must function according to a criterion of sameness within its courts because its judicial goal is primarily justice and fairness. However, to understand what is or is not just or fair in a marriage or couple's relationship when a divorce is initiated, an attorney may be hired to interpret a just and fair separation and equitable distribution of assets. The law does not have the ability or inclination to interpret or assess oneness within the context of the relationship.

Oneness fails when:

- There is no history together so trust can be built
- The engagement period did not include conversations that clarified needs, negotiated expectations, or shared goals
- Two philosophies of lifestyle co-exist independently of one another so there is no foundation on which to build consistency
- Terms used to express feelings have no concrete or shared interpretation
- One partner is in over his or her head in raising and managing children
- There are different spiritual baselines for each partner related to how to meet individual and couples' spiritual needs
- The relationship is built on fantasy rather than reality, causing assumptions rather than facts to be folded into perceived needs, expectations, and goals
- One or both partners feels trapped and controlled and not managed in the relationship

The context of justice and fairness resides within the concept of sameness and their legal definitions and interpretations which, for the most part, continually change over time, incident, and precedent. In the *Rule of Law*, marriages are based on fairness and equity through sameness. In reality, marriage was designed to be either right or wrong and reflected in oneness.

This becomes self-evident when the practitioner and couple embrace the faith-based concept of oneness as their relational goal for implementation of marriage and family processes, including how children and adolescents are raised, managed, and influenced within the family structure.

CHILDREN AND ADOLESCENTS

Parents rarely let go of their children, so children let go of them.
-Mitch Albom

When assessing a family system, the primary adults are the men and women in the marital relationship who bring children—either through childbirth or adoption—into the family unit. While children become adolescents and adult children over time, in this chapter we will focus on young children and adolescents that are controlled and managed by their adult parents. The basic family life cycle addressed through interactional faith-based family therapy encompasses typical patterns of behavior and mental mappings as the family passes through multiple challenges and developmental stages, such as:

- Birth and childhood
- Control and influence across the life span
- Separation from parents
- Marriage and divorce
- Child bearing, tending, and preparation
- Growing older
- Retirement
- Death and bereavement

Awareness of the progressive context of the family helps the practitioner evaluate and normalize the family's presenting problem, dysfunctional behaviors, and faulty mental maps. In the process, family members can achieve a measure of understanding, forgiveness, respect, and restoration of their relationships with one another. Children and adolescents often struggle with their transitions through the early developmental stages of growth and development, particularly if there is disharmony or conflict in the family system.

Children and adolescents—what is the difference?

Various psychotherapists, educators, and practitioners describe the patterns attached to ages of children and adolescents differently. *Children* are generally referred to as minors, human beings living between the stages of conception and birth or infancy through the onset of puberty. The term *minor* is a legal term for a person younger than the age of majority. A child, then is aged 0 to 10 or 13 years and often falls into the following age categories or intervals of growth:

- Fetus: in-utero conception through birth
- Newborn: aged 0 to 4 weeks following birth
- Infant: aged 4 weeks to 1 year
- Toddler (learning to walk): aged 1 to 2 years
- Preschooler (play age): aged 3 to 5 years
- Child school-aged (socialization): 6 to 12 years
- Adolescent (personal identity and independence): aged 13 to 18 or 19 years

- Young person or young adult, beginning with puberty through post-puberty: aged 10 to 13 through 19 to 24 years

Because children grow up, we think a child's purpose is to grow up. But a child's purpose is to be a child. Nature doesn't disdain what only lives for a day. It pours the whole of itself into each moment...Life's bounty is in it's [sic] *flow, later is too late.* —Alexander Herzen

Adolescence is often referred to as the transitional phase between childhood and adulthood, usually between the years of 10 and 18. However, some experts such as the World Health Organization (WHO) set the ages of *adolescents* between 10 and 19 or *young people* between the ages of 10 and 24 years. Characteristics of adolescence include biological markers of increasing growth and development through the years of puberty; advanced decision making and individual assumptions of control; increased pressures from peers, family members, and social influences; and, a search for personal identity and future-oriented goals.

There are certain needs and expectations for families to enable children and adolescents to grow and develop healthy behaviors, purposeful mental maps, and a strong faith. To be successful, they generally need:

- To engage in a functional family unit with biological or adoptive parents or parent surrogates (*e.g.*, grandparents) to experience a sense of love and belongingness (a spiritual need) in a stable, safe, and nurturing family environment

- To experience different levels of learning and communication both inside and outside the home, *e.g.*, school and vocational training or college, as they develop physically, emotionally, socially, cognitively, and spiritually

- To participate in decision making based on level of growth and development in matters directly affecting them to encourage critical thinking and begin exchanging control in childhood for influence in adolescents and young adults

- To be protected from abuse and neglect within the family unit and from harmful influences and exploitation within and outside the family system

- To receive appropriate degrees of discipline and forgiveness to facilitate just and ethical responses to dysfunctional behaviors and faulty mental maps throughout the stages of growth and development

- To be treated with dignity and evolving levels of freedom as they grow beyond parental control into independence and influence in adolescence, developing confidence through encouragement and realization of needs, expectations, and goals

- To develop spiritual strength and identity through faith, forgiveness and hope, connectedness and belonging, and purpose and meaning consistently and conjointly with biological, mental, and emotional stages of growth and development across the life span of childhood and adolescence

The family system is usually comprised initially of the couple alone, adding children who grow into adolescents and young adults and may include elderly parents for one or both couple partners. As the couple ages, the children may eventually become the caregivers of their parents. At times, adults may be caring for elderly parents and children of varied ages, from infancy through young adulthood, sometimes referred to as the *sandwich generation*. Such variations in family units and memberships provide context for faith-based family therapy. It is critical for practitioners to know the structure and influence of each member of the family when identifying problems accurately and planning treatment strategies.

Family structure and influence

Most parents have found that controlling children is the most efficient way to raise them when they have limited time to spend with them. This is effective during the early years, during the time when most parents make all the decisions regarding the child's care and schooling, supporting the child financially, emotionally, physically, and spiritually.

Problems begin to arise when a little switch seemingly tucked deeply in the folds of children's brains shifts into "independent" mode. It automatically engages between the ages of 10 to 12 years and even earlier with some children, a little later with others. This mental apparatus often escapes detection by parents for many reasons, *e.g.*, distractions when caring for their families, managing family and work demands, or attempting to navigate advanced education with work and home responsibilities. However, once it is recognized and understood, closer examination shows it to be an important determinant of the evolving character of each child.

Unfortunately, many parents refuse to acknowledge or accept the reality of its emergence in their children. They attempt to continue controlling their children past the genetically predetermined age of maturation and independence. They then find themselves confronted with rebellion, disrespect, and aggressive behaviors of children struggling with the many changes being experienced in their bodies and ways of thinking. This is sometimes referred to as a *rebellious phase* leading into adolescence and young adulthood. Interestingly, many adults forget how those feelings of independence their children are experiencing felt when they passed through their own years of transitioning into adulthood. They neglect to exchange control for influence (Figure 8.1) as the child ages and begins to develop personal identity and critical thinking in decision making around age-appropriate choices.

Figure 8.1. Exchanging control for influence

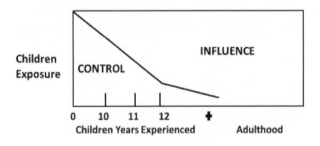

We worry about what a child will become tomorrow, yet we forget that he is someone today. -Stacia Tauscher

Parents who recognize normative developmental phenomenon gradually begin to integrate methods to reduce control, increase personal responsibility, and model gracious acts of kindness whenever faced with their children's growing demands for independence. They gradually exchange control for influence, a process that continues throughout the lives of parents and children. Eventually, parents experience the ability to exert influence in their children's decisions as they release full control to them in adulthood. This results in purposeful and healthy independent adults, ready to assume the responsibilities that come with maturity in thought, faith, and behavior. This type of influence teaches children, adolescents, and young adults what it means to have faith in what is best in most decisions and activities, *e.g.*, faith in their parents' advice, faith that their parents are doing or intending what is best for them and for the family, and faith in what they are observing in their parents behaviors and decisions is trustworthy.

As children mature, parents begin to relinquish their total control of their children's decisions and activities to facilitate and support their evolving independence, increasing their responsibilities, and encouraging their faith and spiritual progress as they grow into adulthood. As they do so, parents steadily exchange control for influence, continually building their sphere of influence over their children's choices, decisions, and activities. This allows children to gradually internalize a sense of personal integrity and accountability as they take risks within the safe context of family, which provides a concrete foundation for learning about faith and folding their faith into their mental maps and behaviors in adolescence and adulthood.

You know children are growing up when they start asking questions that have answers. -John J. Plomp

Once the genetically-driven need for independence is "switched on", the implementation and refinement of influence with children becomes a time and energy-consuming task for parents as the child progresses towards adolescence and young adulthood. As control is incrementally withdrawn, it creates a void that must be filled with influence, guidance, and faith. Children and adolescents continually work through concepts like fairness, sharing, giving instead of taking, and what and how to communicate. They try to rationalize and interpret accurately what they are learning outside of the home with what parents and other family members are teaching them at home. They are connecting to people who may or may not be good role models, emulating behaviors and adopting ways of thinking that may conflict with the beliefs of their parents. Most parents struggle to help their children fill those developmental voids as they precipitously balance their abilities, actions, and beliefs in

- Managing needed control and inserting influence into situations and decisions;

- Determining how and when to control dependence and when to safely encourage autonomy and independent responses to events and ideas;

- Caring for their family relationships and still protecting time for themselves in oneness; and,

- Building faith and hope in their family system to provide a safe and nurturing place for themselves and for all their family members to thrive and grow in heart, mind, habits, and work.

This process of give and take, dependence and independence, and shifting perspectives may continue well into adolescence and young adulthood for some children, who then later become parents struggling to help their children find their way through the confusing and demanding situations they encounter along the way. The acquisition and expansion of personal and a familial faith grounds and enhances the child's maturation over the years as parents value and role model a spiritual reality, nurturing the child's faith along with intellect, behavior, emotions, physical health, and ability to determine right and wrong when making decisions.

Faith-based family practice interventions

The cycle of control creates barriers to managing relationships within the family that continue from generation to generation. The interactional faith-based family practitioner intervenes by helping family members recognize and change patterns of controlling behaviors and ways of thinking that are disrupting their relationships. For example, the practitioner might suggest a parent may take an adult child considering marriage for an outing, *e.g.*, a picnic or day at the beach, to talk to him or her about commitment and marital relationships. They may discuss why the parent married the child's other parent, why they love each other, and the reason for their marital commitment to one another and God as they seek to achieve oneness in their physical, emotional, and spiritual relationships. They may explore how faith within a marriage takes the form of a contractual covenant more than just a simple agreement. Faith is observable and yet a direct influence. Afterwards, the participants may review with the practitioner in session what they learned from their time together and conversations.

While it is possible to teach children table manners at home, for example, it is difficult to remove control from the lesson and to focus on influence. Children often equate home with control until they become confident of their evolving individuality and ability to express their newly emerging independence, and of the interactive give-and-take of influence being modeled by their parents. Realistically, too, parents who attempt to instill influence into their relationships with their children at home frequently encounter too many distractions. The children often do not have their undivided attention. It is easy for parents to then revert to control. Most parents understand control. The role of the practitioner is to teach these critical stages of growth and development—to teach the participant family about influence, not control, as their children incrementally experience varying degrees of independence.

Methods to influence a child, adolescent, or young adult can be creatively designed and implemented at any time and at any age before or after the "independence switch" is engaged. It is important that parents begin by accepting the growing autonomy and rapidly developing individuality of each child as he or she moves towards adolescence and adulthood. Practitioners build homework into their treatment plans and may recommend exercises to facilitate the exchange of control for influence. For example, assigning parents to take a younger child out for a formal dinner in their favorite restaurant. The parents then role model how to act in a public setting, how and what to tip for services rendered, and the flow and elegance of table graces. Demonstrating the characteristics of honesty and stewardship by always checking the receipt when out to eat to make sure waiters or waitresses do not cheat themselves, encouraging the child to emulate these lessons and influencing manners and proper behaviors in the child.

In a time when technology occupies the minds of parents, children, and adolescents, it is easy for parents and children to relinquish their control to computers and other devices that entertain and educate. Such decisions are readily justified when computers are such important tools for work and school assignments. However, taken too far, they become a form of distraction that blocks or ruins opportunities to communicate directly with others, often leading to isolation as people fold themselves into social media and computer games. Instead of connecting to one another and exploring the world through discovery, conflict, chaos, and reason, families can lose themselves and each other in cyberspace. The practitioner might recommend a holiday from technology and have a family that enjoys the outdoors spend a weekend camping. During the time together, they may be asked to complete a set of tasks related to addressing their presenting problem and review their experiences during the next therapy session with the practitioner.

Most parents understand the need to control their children's behaviors and usually believe it to result in a positive influence in how their children act and think. Unfortunately, the reality is that too much control for too long generally creates resentment for most children. The children reflect that resentment through disobedience, anger, rejection, and other acting out behaviors, whether passively (*e.g.*, silence, journaling disappointment, covert disobedience) or actively (*e.g.*, fighting, yelling, overt disobedience). The role of the practitioner is to teach these critical transitions of growth and development—to teach the participant family about influence and control as their children emerge into independence, needing the group support of the family members to do so safely and lovingly. Parenting adults and maturing children require genuine faith in a stable and flexible family system be paramount across the life span.

IN CONCLUSION

The purpose of this book and the therapeutic process methodology is based on the following premise: *The faith of the practitioner working with participants in therapy is caught more than it is taught. Intervening with children, marriage, family, and the progression of maturity is applied learning through a mutually safe and interactive process.*

Families today struggle with rapidly changing sociocultural demands that impact the family system, their relationships, and even how individuals perceive and express their personal identities, *e.g.*, disputing the boundaries of genetics for what is male and female, reconstructing the language for how children and adults express their ideas and beliefs, restructuring what defines a family and renegotiating roles and responsibilities of family members, challenging the beliefs of those who disagree with what was once considered dysfunctional behaviors or faulty mental maps, and disparaging the roles of faith in family systems and members within the family unit.

Men and women struggle with relationships at every age, finding it easier and more socially acceptable to engage in meaningless sexual encounters in sameness rather than in committing to one individual and building oneness for sharing meaningful life experiences and faith. Safety slips away as men present themselves as women and invade the most intimate places where biological women live, work, and heal. Conversely, women believing themselves to be men may place themselves in harm's way by invading the same intimate spaces where biological men live, work, and heal. For example, lawmakers argue about whether a biological woman believing herself to be male should be housed in a men's prison, or if a biological male should be housed in a women's prison. Gender confusion in adults creates confusion and painful choices in family members, especially in children and adolescents. When men and women no longer have a unique identity tied to their genetic codes, X and Y chromosomes, or other biological markers, how can children learn to be healthy adolescent or adult men or women if there is no one to teach them? Where does a practitioner begin when families of faith present with such basic conflicts in themselves, in their children, or in their other family members?

Similarly, many schools are so politicized today, often teaching children and parents to fear to such a degree that drug use, depression, and suicides in young people are skyrocketing. Children are more involved in nihilistic prophecies around debatable ideas about climate change, for example, than in learning how to interact socially and compassionately with one another. "Causes" replace or disrupt studies in history, math, science, language, grammar, computer technology, art, music, and other subjects that used to make up a basic academic curriculum for children and adolescents. Family systems are unable to provide safety or opportunities to challenge the various concepts and ideas they learn in school and work, even those with which they might agree. If parents are so confused about who they are and what they encounter in , how can they help their children learn how to become the men and women God meant them to become?

These are just a few of the many critical challenges families face today. They bring their confusion and conflicts to the faith-based family practitioner for help in finding their way emotionally and spiritually. Presenting problems bring them to therapy and are usually exhibited in troubled behaviors and faulty mental maps, *i.e.*, acting out negatively, suicidal gestures and attempts, disruptive actions during school and at home, *etc.* The key is to discover what is occurring in the family by walking them through the Needs-Expectations-Goals process, refocusing their attention on their family and how their faith strengthens and unites them, and guiding them towards individual health and restoration of familial relationships based on God's absolutes, forgiveness, and grace.

CHAPTER 9:
Faith and Science

Sometimes you put walls up not to keep people out, but to see who cares enough to break them down. -Socrates

DR. HANSEN ON FAITH AND SCIENCE

When it comes to science, I am a lover of the unknown. Furthermore, I don't believe everything should be assessed and integrated to be evaluated. Faith-based family therapy, by its very nature, is a soft (or *qualitative*) science, which assesses individuals not by numerical equivalents or quantities (*quantitative* science) but by qualities or characteristics, for example, the study of the mind (*psychology*) with the emphasis on study.

I have learned over the years that humans have always had the ability to experience change without needing that ability explained them or proven to them through hard, quantitative science. In psychology, the *stimulus-response theory* relates various forms of classical conditioning in which a *stimulus* (an inducement) is paired to a specific response in an individual's mind, becoming part of one's mental mapping process. However, the limited stimulus in such a stimulus-response formula is that it is usually based on the environmental, lacking any other form, context, or reference stimuli.

When there are variables and functional facts that cannot be measured, compared, or tested directly or quantitatively, though, science too often steps away from those realities to verify only what it believes to be proven. In the world of science phenomena, there are diverse anomalies are either not true or not ready to be explained yet scientifically.

Those that know, do. Those that understand, teach. -Aristotle

Practitioners spend a great deal of time assessing and teaching participants about healthy behaviors and mental mapping predicated on cultural, societal, spiritual, and philosophical norms. How, then, does the concept we call *faith* fit into the construct of science? Is it an innate ability folded into a genetic pattern surviving evolution from the beginning like so many other characteristics, *e.g.*, the ability to communicate, determinants for male/female physical qualities, and the DNA (deoxyribonucleic acid) code for how each human being will turn out? Is it an external choice among various options, which may then become genetically relevant to each human who was originally designed by the Creator? How are faith and science aligned with one another in the ethnographic processes relative to the people, culture, traditions, beliefs, habits, and shared differences of participants in faith-based family therapy?

The authors chose to implement focus groups to explore some of these questions qualitatively and to identify opportunities to improve services for faith-based participants struggling to address dysfunctional behaviors and faulty mental maps and to restore broken relationships within their family systems. Let's begin with some speculative observations and then take a closer look at what the focus groups revealed in their studies and applications of interactional faith-based family therapy.

Speculative observations

Science is self-limited by choice, systematically studying physical structures and behaviors through observation and experimentation. Therefore, science can only study what *faith* is without knowing the specifics of who, what, when, where, why, and how. Perhaps faith is built from nothingness stimulated by the environment only. How do participants describe their faith and in what or whom do they place it? For example, is faith grounded in religious beliefs, social expectations, human nature, or environmental consistencies?

With qualitative, ethnographic, phenomenological, quantitative, and triangulated approaches to research design and study, for example, that use multiple ways to collect and assess data on the same topic, process, or quality, science can contribute to the growing body of knowledge related to human behavior and faith-based family therapy. However, in spite of the many approaches and varied designs or overall strategies available for integrating different research variables in a coherent and logical way for study, this ever evolving, multifaceted world struggles with limited measurement tools for definitively assessing, designing, and constructing functional human behavior, thinking, and faith.

When I started out, general science and experimental psychology were my interests. It was the 1960s and quickly began to feel like Pavlov's dog died as the stimulus-response approach to behavioral modification was slowly leaving the world of psychology. My mentor and professor at the time was Leo Baranski. His study of the "Reticular Formation of the Brain as a Central Organizing process" was interesting but controversial. Unfortunately, before he could establish his theories, a lab monkey died and Baranski went into exile as a researcher. It was time for me to consider another course of study.

I decided to pursue a degree in theology. After finishing my graduate studies and theological education, I eased my way back into clinical psychology. Eventually, I determined that systems theory worked best in therapy and started doing Marriage and Family Therapy as a Christian counselor. Folding my education and experience in general science, experimental psychology, clinical psychology, and theology into improving marriage and family therapy, I laid the academic and clinical foundation for interactive faith-based family counseling and therapy. I teamed up with a dear friend and wonderful fellow scholar, Dr. Diana Swihart, to write a book in the early 1990s. This book is an advanced iteration of that work with more tools and details around the science and faith of this interactive approach to family therapy.

To merge a science—even a soft science like psychology—with theology or anything faith-based has been considered by some professionals as lacking in academic precedence. But this has never bothered or deterred me or my co-author. When we speak of interactive family systems therapy, a faith-based approach (the title of our first book and substance of this one), we are representing the following concepts and dynamics:

- *Interaction* represents the family dialog designed to clarify and afford the healing process and restoration of relationships to take place.

- *Family* denotes the ideal that at least two people had to agree to make any changes in life and in the hierarchies of family members.

- *Systems* signifies the environments and structures of people, places, and things affecting change when they are recognized.

- *Therapy* designates an identified and organized theory or technique while orchestrating healthy changes.

- *Faith-based* expresses the trust, commitment, and motivation to change with certainty and a focus.

- *Approach* indicates the strategy of clarity used to validate and implement the therapeutic process.

Throughout this book, each of these elements have been defined, described, and folded into the whole context of interactive faith-based family therapy. These are the same elements and principles introduced to the students engaged in the focus groups, providing a foundation of practice for them to implement the process and evaluate their outcomes. We began by reviewing how to explain faith-based therapy to people of faith presenting for therapy.

FAITH-BASED THERAPY FOR PEOPLE OF FAITH

In the Biblical *parable*, or story, of the farmer scattering seeds, we can learn a great deal about how to grow healthy relationships through the healing process of faith-based family systems therapy:

A farmer went out to plant some seeds. As he scattered them across his field, some seeds fell on a footpath, and the birds came and ate them. Other seeds fell on shallow soil with underlying rock. The seeds sprouted quickly because the soil was shallow. But the plants soon wilted under the hot sun, and since they didn't have deep roots, they died. Other seeds fell among thorns that grew up and choked out the tender plants. Still other seeds fell on fertile soil, and they produced a crop that was thirty, sixty, and even a hundred times as much as had been planted! -Matthew 13.3b-8

Before practitioners place the seeds of therapy into the family garden, they need to intentionally and systematically prepare the ground and the soil for the planting. Growing healthy plants requires cautious planning, careful plowing the field, watering just enough, and energizing and enriching the soil of mental maps before the sowing of seeds planted can happen. And, sometimes, the soil just needs to sit and rest for a while.

In the parable applied to faith-based family therapy, seeds that fell on the footpath represent counseling or advice that is received but not understood, the information or recommendations easily lost when families are exposed to competing demands on their time, energy, and efforts.

Seeds falling in shallow soil or rocky ground are like good intentions to implement the tasks for healing that are readily received but are not followed up—they have no roots and the good intentions quickly disappear. The seeds among the thorns are quickly forgotten or discounted, pushed aside by the worries and fears of life seen in families unwilling to trust one another or to believe that their God can heal them or meet their immediate needs. These are often seen in sessions where it may feel as if some family members are sowing discord, disharmony, or distress.

Practitioners help prepare good soil to receive therapeutic seeds so participants can manage and remove destructive or negative disruptive behaviors revealed during the explorations of their needs, expectations, and goals for therapy. Then, when they have achieved a salubrious balance among their family members, they can begin to reap the harvest of restored relationships with healthier behaviors and greater clarity in new ways of thinking with deeper spiritual discernment and faith.

Spirituality expressed through faith is one of the dimensions of humanity. Carson and Koenig (2008) describe a whole person perspective that speaks to the human spirit housed in a physical body influenced by the environment and external social, cultural, spiritual, and familial stresses. In their conceptual model of the nature of humans, the psychosocial mind, biological body, and spirit are dynamically woven together with each dimension, or part, affecting and being affected by the other dimensions of being:

- *Biological dimension*: five senses, how we access the material world of reality through touch, taste, hear, see, and smell

- *Psychosocial dimension*: interactive influences among will moral sense, intellect, and emotion

- *Spiritual dimension*: God-conscious, relatedness to faith, deity, holiness, how we experience interrelatedness, or integration, through forgiveness, love and belonging, and trust resulting in meaning and purpose and hope

Although the spiritual dimension is a universal dimension within every person, the expression and meaning individuals attribute to spirituality and how they express their faith often differ significantly, even among those within the same family. For example, one member of a family may express his or her spirituality through music or art; another family member may do so through service to the community (*i.e.*, helping the homeless) or the church (*i.e.*, teaching a Sunday School class or being part of the cleaning staff). Some of the emotions or concerns family members may bring to practitioners that indicate they are struggling with issues of faith, for example, might be:

- Anger at God, their church, spiritual leaders, or those who attend religious services
- A sense of abandonment, isolation, or deep-seated loneliness, without love or a sense of belongingness
- A lack of meaning or purpose
- Little or no sense of absolutes, of what is right or wrong (*e.g.*, relativism)
- Loss of personal identity or gender confusion
- Suicidal ideation or gestures
- Feelings of betrayal, lack of forgiveness received or ability to forgive
- Reflecting negatively on personal existence, on the reality of God, questioning need for faith or God, rebelling against God and what they once believed
- Fighting against the values, faith, teachings, behaviors, or beliefs of their families or those of individual members of their families, resulting in aberrant behaviors or faulty mental maps

"*Spirituality* is an elusive word to define. Like the wind, we can see its effects [sic] but we can't grasp it in our hands and hold onto it. We recognize when someone is in "low" or "high" spirits, but is that spirituality? We believe that a patient's quality of life, health, and sense of wholeness are affected by spirituality, yet still we struggle to define it. Why? Most likely because spirituality represents "heart" not "head" knowledge, and "heart" knowledge is difficult to encapsulate in words. Spirituality is described in a variety of ways: as a principle, an experience, a sense of God, the inner person" (Carson & Koenig, 2008, pp 4-5). O'Brien describes spirituality "as a personal concept… generally understood in terms of an individual's attitudes and belief related to transcendence (God) or to the nonmaterial forces of life and of nature" (2003, p 4). Faith is the conduit for the expression of the spiritual dimension of being. Science is unable to observe the spiritual dimension directly and can only speak to the manifestations of faith in the lives of the practitioner, the individual, and members within the family system.

Relationships of faith and scientific inquiry

Science attempts to confirm what is known while affirming consistency, often through replications of data analysis and process outcomes. Science prefers to argue about quantitatively duplicating the stimulus-response factors, for example. However, it is the softer, qualitative sciences such as psychology and phenomenology that can open doors to research in the spiritual dimension of being and how faith interacts with it. Consider how Freud's model of the psyche (the id, ego, and super-ego) is taught in virtually every university psychology and counseling course, though the underlying premises cannot be proven and can be interpreted differently in social and philosophical ways. Yet they have become the root of all modern forms of secular therapy.

Quantitative science depends on an empirical approach limited to the experiential or quasi-experimental designs, for example, and adaptive expectations logic, which supposes expectations of future values of a variable can be based on its values in a recent past. Some researchers in the scientific method believe faith is impossible when imagining any empirical observations, such as the counter-intuitive theories, *e.g.*, the James-Lange theory that emotions are the result of biological or physical changes in the body.

Faith is often considered to be neither falsifiable nor verifiable since it cannot be quantified or "proven" in the first place. An interesting aspect of scientific validation is that faith (or any variable) must be falsified to separate it from anything else. In other words, if something is true, then there needs to be something false with which to compare it. Therefore, proving what is valid and true is necessary when seeking ways to change what is currently believed in order to embrace something new, such as redefining indifferent mental maps about forgiveness, hope, faith, or eternal life. Therefore, science cannot be applied singularly to research involving faith or spirituality.

However, this does not negate the relevancy of faith and its connection to a gestalt personality capable of self-regulation and independent motivation in solving problems as an outpouring of an individual's spiritual dimension of being. Empirical science does not have to prove spirituality or faith for it to be a critical tool in effective therapy for believers and families of faith. For this reason, focus groups were selected to study the effectiveness of faith-based family therapy using a more qualitative approach to inquiry.

FOCUS GROUP CONCEPTS

The power of a focus group lies in its ability to leverage multiple channels of communication and thought. When you buckle down and really explore the many facets of a possible innovation…, you are more able to make well thought-out decisions. -Craig Cochran

The study of faith and the arguments that comprise the doctrines and beliefs from which faith emerges and grows is referred to as *apologetics*, evidences and reasoned arguments or writings in justification of a theory, doctrine, or idea. Faith and religious truth, such as Christianity, is not relegated to the realm of belief alone but is grounded in evidence and reason. John Stonestreet (Wallace, 2017) reminds us that while Christians' deeply held commitments are mere beliefs, those beliefs are based on reality. Faith involves more than knowledge, but it does not involve less. Genuine Christianity (Swihart, 2016) describes reality clearly and challenges believers and skeptics alike to examine everything carefully.

How do practitioners explore such evidences in the field of interactive faith-based family therapy as it folds in family systems theory? Wallace (2017), the author of *Forensic Faith*, encourages investigation into what individuals believed accidently to find evidential certainty for their faith. Many participants who seek family therapy are accidental believers, often accepting whatever spiritual guidance and teachings their family chose without looking at what those teachings might mean to them personally and as family members.

What is a focus group?

Focus groups are groups of usually 6 to 12 individuals brought together in a specific location to engage in guided discussions about an identified topic. The goal of a focus group is to validate or develop possible and current target audience themes or challenges, to gather opinions and attitudes about specified services, concepts, or ideas. Changes in therapeutic practices due to further study can be considered, potentially resulting in a determination to improve or go beyond established postulates.

In general, a focus group is designed to explore baseline issues and gather target audience feedback before deciding on how to further develop or change current practices beyond the existing therapeutic approaches with occasionally unpredictable assumptions caused by any change in process or outcomes. A focus group can ask strategic questions or present new or challenging ideas for discussion to bring credibility and evidence to an individual subject or to validate an interactive approach to faith-based family therapy.

Purpose and rationale for focus groups

The focus group was implemented as a method for authorizing the interactional faith-based approach to family therapy rather than as an integrative approach to unify separate theories or processes. In this way, the final project became more isomorphic, or similar in outcomes, validating a reasonable assumption that significant change occurs with increased clarity and reduced confusion in the NEG process.

It's really hard to design products by focus groups. A lot of times, people don't know what they want until you show it to them. -Steve Jobs

Attempting to pull multiple theories about a given subject or idea into a single universal approach on how to manage therapy generally stalls participant willingness to change behaviors or ways of thinking, adding layers of confusion and conflicting practices. The focus group maintains the idea of possibility and is a method of confirming or validating goals and outcomes at the same time.

1. Psychology and theology have always had opposing views because of having unique inferences. *Therefore*, can inferences in counseling and therapy interrupt the therapeutic process and confuse the results of legitimate change?

2. The faith-based approach has a common "change agent" and is recognized as a major influence in rehabilitation. *Therefore*, can faith be defined as a bridge or gap between theology and psychology if both are interested in change and the unknown focus of unexplained motivation?

3. Faith-based approaches in behavior modification seem to be more progressive and experiential-oriented than they are concerned with past emotional behavior disorders at times. *Therefore*, can belief in something or someone other than one's self stimulate positive change in lifestyle as part of the human spirit and, therefore, within the processes of recognized counseling or therapy?

The authors hold that any attempt to force integration of both cognitive and behavioral outcomes is empirically dishonest.

MANAGING THE PROCESS

Multiple methods are available for collecting and analyzing data from various sources, *e.g.*, focus group discussions, interviews, surveys, document reviews, and direct and indirect observation. The information and intention of this approach was to provide exposure to counseling and therapy opportunities that included the concept of faith in the therapeutic process.

The "faith concept" in faith-based family therapy

Religion is a belief system that influences how participants and practitioners express their spirituality and was not a focus for these groups. *Faith* was defined as any beliefs connected first to the practitioner, which could be transferred from the practitioner to the participant in thought and behavior and provided the foundation for change folded into these therapeutic processes. Assumptions about faith were:

- Faith is a significant part of the natural flow of communication between practitioners and participants in all counseling and therapy endeavors
- Faith is first observed as personal character, which results first in trust and ultimately builds individual and familial confidence
- Faith is an observed process, evidenced by practitioners and by participants
- Faith in therapy represents a belief in a process other than implementation of a planned technique, methodology, or intervention alone
- Faith is not an intergraded (*i.e.*, linked or coordinated) technique but the extended potential inherent in the therapeutic process outcome
- The faith-based approach to doing therapy is not the administration of an empirical tool but a qualitative analysis approach to assessing attitudes demonstrated within the emotional and spiritual dimensions of being
- The faith-based approach is not a trick or gimmick; it is focused human hope introduced by the practitioner into the family system

Faith-based practices require a willingness of practitioners and participants to engage in active listening with one another, to talk about spiritual, physical, emotional, cognitive, and behavioral concerns driving dysfunctions within the family system, and to seek supports for changing problematic actions and ways of thinking through faith and restoration of family relationships. The focus groups explored these possibilities for participants from families of faith.

OVERVIEW OF PROCESS AND ANALYSIS

Focus group research has created a composite No-Man who resembles no-one anyone has ever met. -Cathy Lewis

What did we hope to learn from the focus groups?

- Is faith a motivator for change?

- Is faith a part of what it means to be a human being?

- Is faith observed when modeled by a practitioner?

- Is faith a feeling that can be objectified and measured as to its impact on participant clients?

- Is faith a motivator for change or a prerequisite of what can become a passion for change?

Faith is an individual quality with the potential to call one to a higher purpose, facilitating restoration of broken lives and relationships through sacrifice, love, trust, respect, communication, and understanding among family members through therapeutic interventions.

IN CONCLUSION

The aggregated comments from all the focus groups interviewed and their discussions around the four key questions presented to them resulted in the following summaries:

- **Focus Group Question #1**: There appears to be room to include the concept of faith in the licensing process since faith is not confined to a religion or a group with a specified belief system, thereby focusing on something that might be perceived as exclusive to one group or individual over others.

- **Focus Group Question #2**: Knowing that a practitioner implemented faith-based therapies might cause a non-referral to them. However, networking with such practitioners would be important in knowing how faith is applied to any kind of counseling or therapy for individuals and families of faith.

- **Focus Group Question #3**: A faith-based approach to therapy does not automatically infer a religious imposition or intent to proselytize (*i.e.*, convert or attempt to convert) participants to a particular belief system when practitioners have certifications and legal licensing requirements as part of their skill-sets and endorsements by Rule of Law.

- **Focus Group Question #4**: The faith of the practitioner (counselor or therapist) can influence a participant or participant family for positive and healthy life changes without violating the ethical or legal rights of any individual regardless of their understanding of faith or choices of belief systems.

The focus group discussions and interviews provide a starting point for exploring the role of faith in family therapy. They open the door to further study and improvements in caring for families of faith. When thinking provides clarity, the needs, expectations, and goals of all relationships can be explained and responsibly processed and addressed. Once clarity is acquired, it can be clarified further by using the alternative, the *paradox*, which is sometimes introduced to balance thinking and the decision to continue or terminate clarity in general (appendix G).

EPILOGUE

Attempts at integration will always encourage collaboration.
-Dale F. Hansen

The authors of this book have in God and have accepted Jesus Christ as their personal savior. They believe they were reconciled to God by faith in Jesus and that faith gives them eternal life with God and Christ for Eternity. We, as authors, believe in the promises found in the Bible and that the Word of God changes people's lives. Thank you for considering our personal faith.

What does the Lord require of you but to do justice, to love kindness, and to walk humbly with your God. -Micah 6.8

This book was written for mental healthcare providers and practitioners in counseling and family therapy. It was designed to teach the practitioner how to think and not necessarily what to think. To think paradoxically and "outside the box" requires freedom to explore and discover new ways of thinking and being. The best advice one can give those practicing therapeutic interventions in family counseling and therapy is to reach outside of themselves, fold faith and wisdom into their sessions—and to do so vigorously and with passion.

The pragmatics of human communication become far more effective when they include faith, especially, when shifting the focus of therapy from the interpersonal to the intrapersonal. Genuine communication acts as the vehicle creating the interaction while faith leads the way to epistemological changes in behaviors and mental maps related to problematic or incomplete knowledge, *e.g.*, in therapeutic and phenomenological methodologies, validity, scope, and distinctions between justified beliefs and personal or professional opinions. In essence, it is moving beyond treating humanity as social animals and recognizing the divine in their DNA.

The 1960s signaled a shift in mental healthcare practice from treating the individual to analyzing the intrapersonal, changing the language, *e.g.*, *symptoms* became *problems* and psychodynamics were folded into Family Systems. Interactional pragmatics in communication was born into the field of therapy and counseling. The ideas of Gregory Bateson's research group with Jay Haley, John Weakland, Paul Watzlawick, Don Jackson, and others became the new norm in practice as they adapted some of their processes for faith-based therapy.

It is important for practitioners to possess more than a minimal awareness of past human communication in compliance with scientific studies, though they are limited by their own language and premises. God and faith are rational, supported by external and internal evidences, and offer real support and change in a very complex world.

Wallace (2017) reminds that agreement is often confused with *tolerance*, which is often defined as the idea that all views or opinions have the same or equal merit—that all truth is relative, that no idea, opinion, or belief should be considered more right, acceptable, or important than any other idea, opinion, or belief. Christians are often seen as intolerant because of their belief in absolute Truth and disagreement with many spiritual and ethical arguments considered true and acceptable by popular culture today. However, *classic tolerance* is about embracing a fair, objective, and permissive attitude towards all ideas, opinions, beliefs, traditions, races, religions, and nationalities without allowing them to subsume or negate one's own ideas, opinions, or beliefs.

Practitioners often have thoughtful disagreements with participants. They tolerate one another by maintaining their disagreements or coming to a compromise in agreement, *e.g.*, of the process for healing broken relationships within the family system, homework assignments, and how sessions will proceed. If the disagreement extends to fundamental beliefs or process, practitioners will usually refer the participants to other practitioners or mental healthcare providers. Practitioners assess and address the dysfunctional behaviors and faulty mental maps impacting familial relationships and processes. The goal is to help the family become whole and functional, not to proselytize or debate the participant members or to bring them into lock-step or total agreement with the practitioner or with one another. Tolerance, science, morality, meaning and purpose need to be a part of every practice when engaging in faith-based interactional family therapy to be successful.

The domain of science

Someday, after we have mastered the winds, the waves, the tides, and gravity, we shall harness for God the energies of love. Then, for the second time in the history of the world [humanity] *will have discovered fire.*
-Teilhard de Chardin

Since humanity's existence began, there have been diverse speculations about the origins of anything considered to be outside individual and social relations or observable empirical evidences. The primary speculation insists that only those origins considered measurable using acceptable research factors could be accepted as truth, reality, or socially acceptable behaviors or ideas. Keeping therapy in the domain of science alone forces practitioners to stay within the limits set by their perceived abilities and the abilities of others to repeat or predict their actions to achieve any possibility of cognitive or behavioral change.

Watzlawick, Bavelas, and Jackson (2011) believe "Man cannot go beyond the limits set by his own mind... the mind [can only] study itself..." Therefore, this belief alone, according to some scholars, is actually a statement of faith, indicating that man could exist in the broad, complex, and unrestricted aspects of physical life if he did not limit himself mentally. Wallace further noted that to evaluate the scientific evidence properly, two points are important to keep in mind (2017, p. 207):

1. Science does not 'say' anything. Scientists do. If the scientists evaluating the evidence reject the existence of God before they start, they will never interpret the evidence fairly, even if the evidence points to God as the best explanation.

2. An over-reliance on science is self-defeating. When people say, "Science is the only way to know the truth," they are making a *philosophical* (rather than *scientific*) claim that cannot be tested or discovered with science.

Theology opens the door to multiple possibilities and consequences related to unknown entities and the effects of faith on movements and causes which are sometimes used to justify the need for different kinds of spirits that could corrupt, repair, or change the world. For example, many people believe in angels and demons who are blamed for the blessings or curses endured by their families. Such beliefs and the evidence—or lack of evidence—supporting them are open for discussion during therapy sessions in faith-based family practice. Often, disruptive and troublesome spirits can be replaced by faith in God and confidence in His love and healing. Theistic beliefs encourage practitioners and participants to discover the immutable laws governing all of existence, including the hearts and minds of every person entering therapy based on empirical and phenomenological evidences.

The domain of morality

The Serenity Prayer:
God, give us grace to accept with serenity the things that cannot be changed,
Courage to change the things which should be changed, and the Wisdom to
distinguish the one from the other. -Reinhold Niebuhr

Life, death, sickness, pain, loss, and discomfort demand a realistic form of interactive communication based on intentional, active listening. "I don't know" is important but never enough. People enter counseling and therapy seeking answers they cannot find elsewhere, not in their homes, churches, or support groups, for example. God is not Someone or something to be measured directly using currently acceptable research techniques. Most academics would admit that humanity has the tendency to hypostatize, *i.e.*, to treat or represent abstractions as concrete reality, which is susceptible to superstition, fear, awe, respect, dismissal, or even rejection of a Higher Power, however they might define it.

Where, then, does morality or moral guidelines come from? Who decides? Morality is predicated on a system of values, ethics, beliefs, principles of conduct, laws, and ways of thinking belonging to the members of a particular society or group of individuals, *e.g.*, Christians and atheists hold different beliefs related to the reality and presence of God. Morality encompasses the core principles by which people distinguish right and wrong, good or bad, acceptable or nonacceptable, legal or illegal, normal or abnormal, and so on. There is no way for practitioners to explain morality outside of a social, ethical, theological, or legal context independent of chance, God, or faith. When using the pragmatics of human communication and interactional family therapy to care for families of faith, intrinsic and shared morality is an important determinant for therapy. Christians, for example, generally base their morality and primary therapeutic decisions on the lessons, truths, and absolutes recorded in Scripture, often gleaning examples from their lived experiences within the context of their own societal norms and laws. Practitioners in faith-based family therapy draw on therapeutic interventions available from science, psychology, theology, ethics, and faith that offer strength, understanding, hope, and restoration to families of faith, recognizing and respecting the unique qualities of participants' beliefs and moral choices. Evidence of the moral value of this therapeutic approach can be seen in behavioral and cognitive changes bringing families back together, restoring broken relationships, and healing damaged people.

The domain of meaning and purpose

> For everything its season, and for everything under heaven its time:
> a time to be born and a time to die, a time to plant and a time to uproot,
> a time to kill and a time to heal, a time to pull down and a time to
> build up, a time for mourning and a time for dancing, a time for silence
> and a time for speech. -Ecclesiastes 3.1-7

This brings us back to one of the key spiritual needs every person has, regardless of ethnicity, religion, nationality, ideology, gender, or age: meaning and purpose. Where do practitioners and participants find meaning and purpose within the context of family therapy? Researchers in psychodynamics, for example, purpose to gather data to inform their studies and, potentially, give meaning to current and future therapeutic practices. For people of faith, purpose and meaning expand to incorporate special events, or passions. Researchers, practitioners, participants, *i.e.*, people of faith seek meaning and purpose in their work, daily activities, studies, service, and relationships to discover peace and forgiveness of the past, present and future hope and belongingness, individual resourcefulness and a healthy sense of self, and confidence in God and the power of their faith in managing their own lives and relationships.

Practitioners in faith-based family therapy frequently discuss the meaning or purpose of illness, belief and faith, religious values or ideologies, fears of death or dying, attitudes about giving and receiving love, the purpose of meditation or quiet reflection, forgiveness, hope, the role of

God in illness and dysfunction, the reality of an engaged or distant God, anger or disappointment in God, disagreements within families about the purpose or meaning of faith, and so on (Carson & Koenig, 2008). Generally, participants introduce the focus of their concerns about meaning and purpose troubling them or believed to be impacting their familial relationships.

Without an intrinsic sense of meaning and purpose, there could be very little if any creativity folded into spiritual activities often expressed through culture, faith, and change. The lack of creativity can stagnate the internalized flow of thought and behavior, causing meaning and purpose to be lost or subsumed by life's more mundane or tedious demands and obligations. Practitioners can help participants find their own creativity when experiencing the activities and faith defining their lives and relationships, enabling them to make the changes necessary to achieve that meaning and purpose through interactive faith-based family therapy.

In shifting paradigms from biological and psychological observations to an expanded purpose integrating the spiritual dimension and faith factors, therapy offers hope and an opportunity to heal and change cognitive and behavioral problems to resolve pain and relational conflicts. Hope as a genuine promise is a mandatory shift in an otherwise limited process for practitioners to delicately advance. Fatalism without choice is a destructive counterapproach or response. Believing only in chance or in an unknowable mystery of change limited by the beliefs of those recognizing physical life ends for everyone can disrupt or eliminate progress for those participants seeking positive hope, forgiveness, meaning, purpose, and belongingness.

Unlike the rationale of limited or no hope, faith continuously works for practitioner and participant alike. It confirms the basics of interactional faith-based family therapy:

- We **NEED** God, and

- God **EXPECTS** us to accept His Gift, of reconciliation, and

- We are to have as a primary **GOAL** to serve Him.

IN CLOSING

Action springs not from thought, but from a readiness for responsibility.
-Dietrich Bonhoeffer

Faith is what captures our ability to change without the guarantee of a healthy commitment to secular rational thought or psychology. People are not always rational, but they are usually curious. They experience variable levels of subjectivity in their personal perspectives, experiences, and relationships. Faith is not a realm separate or incompatible with evidence and reason. It is knowable and vital to human wellbeing. Practitioners help participants in faith-based family therapy look at the facts of their behaviors and ways of thinking, considering carefully the dysfunction in their actions and faulty constructs of mental maps that interfere with their abilities to engage in healthy relationships.

BIBLIOGRAPHY

- Ackerman, C. (April 7, 2019). *19 narrative therapy techniques, interventions + worksheets* (pdf). PositivePsychology.com. Retrieved from https://positivepsychology.com/narrative-therapy/.

- Black, J.S., & Gregersen, H.B. (2008). *It starts with one: Changing individuals changes organizations.* Upper Saddle River, NJ: Prentice Hall Pearson Education, Inc.

- Boghossian, P.G. (2013). *A manual for creating atheists.* Durham, NC: Pitchstone Publishing.

- Bowen, M. (1993, 1978). *Family therapy in clinical practice.* New York, NY: Jason Aronson.

- Bullock, M., & Sangeeta, P. (2003). Ethics for all: Differences across scientific society codes. *Science and Engineering Ethics, 9*(20):159-170.

- Cag, P., & Acar, N.V. (2015). A view of the symbolic-experiential family therapy of Carl Whitaker through movie analysis. *Educational Sciences: Theory & Practice, 15*(3):575-586.

- Carson, V.B., & Koenig, H.G. (Eds.). (2008). *Spiritual dimensions of nursing practice* (rev. ed.). West Conshohocken, PA: Templeton Science & Religion, Templeton Foundation Press.

- Couros, G. (Jan 27, 2013). *The principle of change: 5 characteristics of a change agent.* Retrieved from https://georgecouros.ca/blog/archives/3615.

- Csikszentmihalyi, M. (1990). *Flow: The psychology of optimal experience.* NY, NY: HarperCollins.

- Csikszentmihalyi, M. (1996). *Creativity: the psychology of discovery and invention.* NY, NY: HarperCollins.

- Doring, M. (2017). A very brief introduction to choice theory. *Science & Tech.* Retrieved from https://www.headstuff.org/topical/science/psychology/brief-introduction-choice-theory/.

- Essays, UK. (November 2018). *Framo and Inter-generational Family Therapy.* Retrieved from https://www.ukessays.com/essays/psychology/framo-and-intergenerational-family-therapy-psychology-essay.php?vref=1.

- Fisch, R., Weakland, J., & Segal, L. (1982). Brief therapy, the art of causing change quickly. *The Tactics of Change.* San Francisco, CA: Jossey-Bass.

- Friedman, E.H. (1991). Bowen theory and therapy. In A.S. Gurman & D.P. Kniskern (Eds.), **Handbook of Family Therapy,** 2:134-170. Philadelphia, PA, US: Brunner/Mazel.

- Gladding, S.T. (2004). G. Sheppard: What is counselling? A search for a definition. *Notebook on Ethics, Legal Issues, and Standards for Counsellors.* In Counseling: A Comprehensive Profession (5th ed.). Upper Saddle River, NJ: Merrill/Prentice Hall. Retrieved from https://www.ccpa-accp.ca/wp-content/uploads/215/05/NOE.What-is-Counselling-A-Search-for-a-Definition.pdf.

- Gowdy, T. (2020). *Doesn't hurt to ask: Using the power of questions to communicate, connect, and persuade.* NY, NY: Crown Forum.

- Gray, J. (2012). *Men are from Mars, women are from Venus.* NY, NY: HarperCollins Publishers.

- Griffin, W.A. (1993). *Family therapy: Fundamentals of theory and practice*. New York, NY: Brunner/Mazel Publication.

- Griffin, W.A., & Greene, S. (1999). *Models of family therapy: The essential guide*. Philadelphia, PA: Brunner/Mazel Publication.

- Haley, J. (1987). *Structural family therapy, techniques of how to do therapy. Problem-Solving Therapy*. San Francisco, CA: Jossey-Bass.

- Hereford, Z. (n.d.). Healthy personal boundaries & how to establish them. *Essential Life Skills*. Retrieved from https://www.essential-lifeskills.net/personalboundaries.html.

- Hwang, J. (2001). *A reading of pragmatics and paradox*. Retrieved from http://www.mathcs.duq.edu/~packer/Methods/Hwang_Methods.pdf.

- Kanchwala, H. (23 Apr 2019). James-Lange theory of emotion—Decoding the counter-intuitive theory of emotion. Update retrieved from https://www.scienceabc.com/humans/what-is-james-lange-theory-of-emotion.html.

- Keller, W. P. (1983). *Lessons from a sheep dog*. Dallas, TX: Word Publishing.

- Lebow, J.L., et al. (2017). *Milan systemic family therapy*. Chapter, Pietro Barbetta. Springer International Publishing AG. Retrieved from ResearchGate.

- Levant, R. (1984). *Family therapy: A comprehensive overview*. Englewood Cliffs, JN: Prentice Hall.

- Mahrer, A.R. (2004). *The complete guide to experiential psychotherapy*. Boulder, CO: Bull Publishing.

- Mann, D. (2010). *Gestalt therapy: 100 key points*. New York, NY: Routledge Publishing.

- Maxwell, J.C. (2000). *Failing forward: Turning mistakes into stepping stones for success.* Nashville, TN: Thomas Nelson, Inc. Amazon Digital Services, LLC.

- Meehl, P., et al (1958). *What, Then, Is Man?* St. Louis, MO: Concordia.

- Mental Research Institute (MRI): Available at https://mri.org/.

- Mills, J. (Jan 2010). *Object relations theory.* Retrieved from https://www.researchgate.net/publication/314045956_Object_Relations_Theory.

- Milton, J. (2014). *Making sense of psychotherapy and psychoanalysis.* London E15 4BQ: British Psychoanalytic Council and Mind Publications. Retrieved from: www.bpc.org.uk/sites/psychoanalytic-council.org/files/Mind-opt.pdf.

- Minuchin, S., & Fishman, H.C. (1981; 2009). Structural family therapy, family systems for change. *Family Therapy Techniques.* Harvard University Press. Amazon Digital Services, LLC.

- Minuchin, S., Reiter, M.D., & Borda, C. (2014). *The craft of family therapy: Challenging certainties* (S. A. Walker, R. Pascale & H. T. M. Reynolds, Contributors). New York, NY, US: Routledge/Taylor & Francis Group. Retrieved from https://psycnet.apa.org/record/2013-42257-000.

- Monty Pelerin's World. (2019). *182 Paraprosdokians.* Retrieved from http://www.economicnoise.com/2011/09/05/182-paraprosdokians/. (Note: Many of these are repeated in this listing—there are only about 80 unique examples provided.)

- Newell, J. (Spring 2019). Where psychology meets spirituality. *Biola, A Voice of Freedom.* La Miranda, CA: Biola University; 30-33.

- Roth, J.W. (Ed.). (2015). *Core curriculum for preceptor advancement.* Peyton, CO: American Academy for Preceptor Advancement.

- Satir, V., Banmen, J., Gerber, J., & Gomori, M. (1991). *The Satir model: Family therapy and beyond.* Palo Alto, CA: Science & Behavior Books.

- Schaller, L.E. (1978). *The change agent: The strategy of innovative leadership.* Nashville, TN: Abingdon.

- Shelly, J.A., John, S.D., & Others. (1983). *Spiritual dimensions of mental health.* Downers Grove, IL: Intervarsity Press.

- Stoll, R. I. (1989). The essence of spirituality. In V. B. Carson (ed.), *Spiritual Dimensions of Nursing Practice.* Philadelphia: W. B. Saunders Company.

- Swihart, M. (2016). *Christianity simplified: The basics of the Christian faith for new believers and curious nonbelievers.* Portland, OR: Third Day Publishing.

- Swihart, D., & Figueroa, S. (2014). *The preceptor program builder: Essential tools for a successful preceptor program.* Danvers, MA: HCPro.

- Tanzi, D. (2015). Chapter 9. Communication. In *Core Curriculum for Preceptor Advancement* by J.W. Roth (Ed.). Peyton, CO: American Academy for Preceptor Advancement.

- USLegal, Inc. online definition at https://definitions.uslegal.com/f/family.

- Wallace, J.W. (2017). *Forensic faith: A homicide detective makes the case for a more reasonable, evidential Christian faith.* Colorado Springs, CO: Davide C Cook; East Sussex, England: David C Cook UK Kingsway Communications.

- Watzlawick, P., Bavelas, J.B., & Jackson, D.D. (2011). *Pragmatics of human communication: A study of interactional patterns, pathologies and paradoxes.* New York, NY: W.W. Norton & Company.

- Watzlawick, P., Weakland, J., & Fisch, R. (1974). Change and its relationship to therapy. *CHANGE, principles of problem formation and problem resolution*. Newton and Company.

APPENDICES:

APPENDIX A.
NEEDS CLARIFICATION WORKSHEET

NEEDS CLARIFICATION WORKSHEET	
I need	so I can
I need	so I can
I need	so I can
I need	so I can
I need	so I can
I need	so I can
I need	so I can
I need	so I can
I need	so I can
I need	so I can
I need	so I can
I need	so I can
I need	so I can
I need	so I can
I need	so I can
I need	so I can
I need	so I can
I need	so I can

APPENDIX B.
NEGOTIATED EXPECTATIONS WORKSHEET

NEGOTIATED EXPECTATIONS WORKSHEET			
I expect	(name)	to (do something)	and in turn, I will
I expect		to	and in turn, I will
I expect		to	and in turn, I will
I expect		to	and in turn, I will
I expect		to	and in turn, I will
I expect		to	and in turn, I will
I expect		to	and in turn, I will
I expect		to	and in turn, I will
I expect		to	and in turn, I will
I expect		to	and in turn, I will
I expect		to	and in turn, I will
I expect		to	and in turn, I will
I expect		to	and in turn, I will
I expect		to	and in turn, I will

APPENDIX C.
NEGOTIATED EXPECTATIONS WORKSHEETS: MARRIAGE

Negotiating reasonable expectations in MARRIAGE	
I expect my spouse to:	_____ and in turn I will _____ _____ (add spouse's need) _____ _____ _____ _____
I expect my spouse to:	_____ and in turn I will _____ _____ (add spouse's need) _____ _____ _____ _____
I expect my spouse to:	_____ and in turn I will _____ _____ (add spouse's need) _____ _____ _____ _____
I expect my spouse to:	_____ and in turn I will _____ _____ (add spouse's need) _____ _____ _____ _____
I expect my spouse to:	_____ and in turn I will _____ _____ (add spouse's need) _____ _____ _____ _____

APPENDIX D.
NEGOTIATED EXPECTATIONS WORKSHEETS:
RELATIONSHIPS

Negotiating reasonable expectations in a RELATIONSHIP	
I expect (this person)	(name) _____ to _____ _____ _____ and in turn I will _____ _____ _____ _____ (help him/her meet his/her relational need) _____ _____ _____
I expect (this person)	(name) _____ to _____ _____ _____ and in turn I will _____ _____ _____ _____ (help him/her meet his/her relational need) _____ _____ _____
I expect (this person)	(name) _____ to _____ _____ _____ and in turn I will _____ _____ _____ _____ (help him/her meet his/her relational need) _____ _____ _____
I expect (this person)	(name) _____ to _____ _____ _____ and in turn I will _____ _____ _____ _____ (help him/her meet his/her relational need) _____ _____ _____

APPENDIX E.
SETTING GOALS WORKSHEET

SETTING GOALS WORKSHEET			
Type of Goals	**Directions:** Precise statement of what you feel is necessary to be accomplished in fulfilling the total purpose for each set of goals	**Proposed date**	**Actual date**
Individual goals			
Relationship goals			
Family goals			

APPENDIX F.
EXAMPLES OF COUNSELING TECHNIQUES

EXAMPLE OF A TASK IN COUNSELING. Tasks are different than making assignments in that they are active and require physical effort.

The father of a teenager is concerned his son has a curfew of 9:00 pm on school nights or to call if he is going to be late getting home.

> "*Therapist*: If your son is not home or has not called by 9:00 then you are to go out looking for him."

> "*Father*: I have to go to work in the morning."

> "*Therapist*: To show you care about him plan your search to include driving by his friends' homes and places your son frequents."

The son was embarrassed to know his father was looking for him and after a week and a half he called every time if he was going to be late. In completing the task, the father also met his need and accomplished his goal to protect his family.

EXAMPLE OF AN ASSIGNMENT IN COUNSELING. Assignments are different than tasks in that they are thoughtful and require an effort to express a thought.

A husband was late for the evening family meals on a regular basis. His wife and the children would wait for his arrival in order to eat together as a family. His wife was overwhelmed with all of the different schedules and the timing for each family member.

> "Therapist: Your assignment for the next two weeks is to call 30 minutes before dinner time to announce your arrival every day late or not late."

"*Husband*: How does that help the daily stress my wife is experiencing?"

"*Therapist: The phone call accomplishes two things: first arrival time and secondly lets you know how her day is going before you get home.*"

The wife was appreciative of the arrival time and the attempt to understand how her day was going. In completing the assignment, the wife could make adjustments to the schedule and receive a message of the husband's awareness and understanding of her pressure. As counselor we give assignments to build self-confidence, which was one of his needs. A "win-win" situation.

EXAMPLE OF COMPLIANCE IN COUNSELING. Being in compliance means following up with past agreements that require honorable acceptance in future endeavors.

A woman found herself to be a fantastic shopper, coupon clipper, and buyer of just about everything on sale. But her husband complained about the amount she was spending with his agreement to spend money. She insisted he did not appreciate her ability to find bargains.

"*Therapist*: As a new wife did you ever honor a certain amount you wouldn't spend without both of you giving mutual consent? Many times there is an amount but not necessarily stated"

"*Woman:* Are you saying my husband does not trust me spending and saving money in this way?"

"*Therapist*: I am saying your husband views your bargain hunting as out of compliance and not out of control of mutual responsibility.

"*Woman:* So what do I do now?"

"*Therapist*: Get in compliance"

The woman not only became compliant with her husband but they both agreed she had a need to start a business of her own and set a goal to start formal education toward becoming a purchasing agent. Being out of control was not the issue.

EXAMPLE OF CHANGE IN COUNSELING. Faith-based Change is different than a change in *status quo* in life and behavior and requires change for change sake.

A married couple was having issues of trust and concerns involving faithfulness. The wife felt her husband looked at other women when they went to the fitness center and the husband felt there were innuendos his wife would be moving out if there was any unfaithfulness. The husband came from a dysfunctional family.

> "*Therapist*: What makes you suspicious of each other?"
>
> "*Husband*: She might leave."
>
> "*Wife*: He might cheat"
>
> "*Therapist*: If your wife leaves would you then cheat?"
>
> "*Husband*: No!"
>
> "*Therapist*: Other than the husband having a bad habit is there any reasons confirming the husband is not being faithful?"
>
> "*Wife*: No!"
>
> "*Therapist*: Suspicions are based on facts not on feelings. As an individual you are to record all facts pertaining to appreciation and respect."

This was a *Paradigm Shift* based on reasonable facts causing change because the assumptions were causing confusion and distractions. The Paradigm Shift is the most stable reason for making a change when use correctly.

APPENDIX G.
PRAGMATIC PARADOX IN SESSION

The pragmatic paradoxical approach to the interactional process for faith-based family therapy focuses on choices in life and the freedom to manage them. It fits well with the themes noted by Dr. Hansen from interviews and focus group discussions. The objective of this therapeutic approach is to rethink the way practitioners think and engage participants by combining *Rational Emotive Behavior Therapy* (REBT) with *Family Systems Therapy*. Practitioners reason once through the NEG process. If no change is experienced, the *Paradox* begins; but, this time practitioners moved backward from the GOALS, then to EXPECTATIONS, and finally NEEDS to make it PARADOXICAL.

Phase I: (Pre-paradoxical)

- Clearly identify individual NEEDS and clarify them for recognition of personal boundaries and values.

- Identify 4 or 5 EXPECTATIONS and negotiate them, avoiding demands and ultimatums.

- Set GOALS for direction rather than accomplishments regarding individual (personal) and familial relationships (others).

- Responses collected for motivation identifying as PASSIONS.

Phase II: (Paradoxical)

Developing the creative process of PARADOXICAL application by returning to Phase I and adding choices on what is flexible and absurd in its GEN interpretation working from the Goals, to the Expectations, and then to the Needs. The decision to continue any relationship or terminate is the responsibility of the participant(s). This becomes clearer when sequencing the NEG process.

Sequence Clarification of the NEG Process

I. SEQUENCE OF PROCESS

- **NEEDS** (*Values* and *Boundaries*) – Avoid WANTS

  I need _____ so I can _____

  I need _____ so I can _____

  I need _____ so I can _____

- **EXPECTATIONS** (*Communication* and *Commitment*) –Avoid Demands and Ultimatums

  I expect _____ and in turn I will _____

  I expect _____ and in turn I will _____

  I expect _____ and in turn I will _____

- **GOALS** (*Direction* for developing Passion) – Give direction only

  In months I will accomplishes the following goal:.

  In months I will accomplish the following goal: .

  In months I will accomplish the following goal: .

- **MOTIVATION.** Energy to *clarify* NEEDS, *negotiate* EXPECTATIONS, and *set* GOALS. Part of the end result of the process identifies the PASSION to change.

  I get excited about doing _____ in life.

II. PRAGMATIC PARADOXICAL, if needed, reverse the process to GEN approach based on the negative process.

APPENDIX H.
Q&A: A FAITH-BASED APPROACH TO FAMILY THERAPY

QUESTIONS	ANSWERS
How do you know human beings have the capacity to have faith and an inherited ability to believe and have "faith" available to make changes while they are exposed to life experiences?	The beginnings of the life of a human being is either an accident or made possible by design. Even if chance is involved, it had to be materialized from other prior existing living matter. On the other hand, there can be a "designer" or Creator God who designed, directed, and made the motivation of "faith" by design. Scientist tell us that the human brain is barely used which leaves room in that design what can generate "faith" as a factor unlike the animal kingdom
The Christian Bible says in 2 Timothy 3:16-17 that "*Reproof for correction*" is the biblical way to counsel. So why does it not suffice that we only use Scripture and the Holy Spirit to help with those who are suffering with anxiety, depression, and stress?	That part of Scripture was written by the Apostle Paul while in jail at the end of his ministry for teaching and possibly for Christians in recovery but not in the beginning stages of unbelievers in recovery. Correction implies that there was a specific deviation from a previous path. Therapy seeks prepare for a different way of approaching life.
Is therapy that is not biblical a sin if you are a believer?	Therapy in its purest form like Music is AMORAL. Therapy is related to feelings and Theology is related to facts. Faith built on fact and therapy is built on feelings.
Can a therapist who is not faith-based do therapy with someone who is faith-based?	Yes, human behavior and cognitive constructs have commonalities which all therapists have studied. As attitudes differ so also does faith as an interpersonal approach to doing the work of a therapist.

Can faith-based approaches to doing therapy be harmful to counselees if it fails to bring changes in behavior?	No, Faith goes beyond the process of change to answer the "why" questions which most therapists attempt to avoid in interactional family therapy.
Can faith interfere with realistic changes in the family or individual?	Yes, faith is a matter of purpose and fact to most believers and if that faith is the result of false doctrine and dogma.
As a Christian, how should I choose between a biblical approach to counseling and psychotherapy?	When unsure, choose someone who is State licensed as a counselor or therapist. Pastoral counselors can teach biblical insight in what God would expect and most likely would provide, protect, and safely explore options while being held accountable for ethically conducting themselves ethically.
How do I find a state licensed counselor or therapist that compliments my faith in God?	Ask